Compliments of
ADM Investor Services

MARKETING BOOT CAMP

85 Profit-Packed Tools, Techniques & Strategies To Boost Your Bottom Line . . . NOW!

by

Arnold Sanow

J. Daniel McComas

KENDALL/HUNT PUBLISHING COMPANY
4050 Westmark Drive   Dubuque, Iowa 52002

Here Is What Others Are Saying This Book Will Do For YOU:

"Whether you work from the kitchen table or the conference table, *Marketing Boot Camp* is a must *have!*"

— **Jill Jensen, Edmund Petersen,** Hosts of television show "Home Business" on National Empowerment Television, (NET)

"The secret of business success has always been successful marketing, but it is a secret revealed when you read *Marketing Boot Camp.* The strategies are classic, but you will learn tactics and applications that are musts for today's computer/space age era. You can't afford to be without these modern tools."

— **Herman Holtz,** Author of *The Consultant's Guide to Winning Clients* and *The Direct Marketer's Workbook*

"We were amazed at how quickly we could achieve results from the strategies in the book. On the same day that we decided to employ some of these techniques, we found an opportunity that should be worth thousands of dollars over the next few months."

— **Ronald Baras,** President, Computer Training Company

"This book is the next best thing to having your own Marketing Director. It makes marketing easy to understand and even easier to do."

— **Denise Dudley,** Executive Vice President, Co-Owner, SkillPath Seminars, Author of *Every Woman's Guide to Career Success*

"*Marketing Boot Camp* provides the competitive advantages your business needs in order to survive and prosper in today's marketplace."

— **Edward Segal,** President, Edward Segal Communications

"If you've been looking for an effective and economical *system* for getting new business and keeping it, this book will get you there faster than any resource I know."

— **Michael Audy Houle,** President, Senior Creative Officer, New Planet Studios

"The authors' work in marketing our business has made an impactful and lasting impression on helping our company grow into what it is today."

— **Robert Felton,** President, Certified Learning Centers, Inc.

"*Marketing Boot Camp* is a 'proactive book.' It makes you think as you read. And if you apply just one of the ideas, you'll end up enjoying business a bit more, and achieve greater business success. I'm a professional marketer, and this book gave me new ideas."

— **Andrew D. Gilman,** President of CommCore, Inc. and Co-author of *Get to the Point*

"If your top priority is your bottom line, you need this book."

— **Jeff Bush,** Marketing Consultant, First Flight Marketing Publications

"Our business is growing fast. *Marketing Boot Camp* is just what we need to help us generate larger clients with more interesting and challenging assignments."

— **George and Nancy Eade,** Creative Director and President, Eade Creative Services

"The authors have done it again! Not only have their workshops and seminars helped me to boost my profits, but the invaluable information in *Marketing Boot Camp* is now right at my fingertips."

— **Bill Vanderbilt,** President and Editor of *The Wedding Pages*

"*Marketing Boot Camp* is more than a book. It provides you with a step-by-step strategy to help you cut costs, increase profits and give you that extra winning edge."

— **Lynn Waymon,** Co-author of *Great Connections: Small Talk and Networking for Business People*

"*Marketing Boot Camp* is one of the most innovative, practical, easy to read books that is must reading for anyone who wants to make it in a challenging world."

> — **Patricia Fripp,** CPAE, Past President, National Speakers Association and Author of *Get What You Want*

"I've seen the authors in action on the platform. Now I'm delighted to see their sage marketing advice in print. If you want to sell more of your products and services, this book will open your eyes to a whole new world of profit possibilities."

> — **Barbara Baker,** Publisher, "Washington Business Advisor"

"The practical no-nonsense guide to what really works in marketing."

> — **Fred Berns,** Author of *Free Publicity! How to Get Quoted and Promoted in the Media*

"Extremely helpful advice to get better results from your marketing and cut costs at the same time."

> — **Jay McNulty,** Owner, Natural Bodies Fitness Center

We Dedicate This Book To Your Prosperity,
And The Prosperity Of Your Clients And Customers

Table of Contents

SECTION 4: Golden Keys To Making More Sales

SECTION 5: Keeping Customers Coming Back

Foreword

You can have the best product or service in the world, but without a well-conceived marketing strategy, your chances of success become slim.

The problems most entrepreneurs face is that they don't have the time or inclination to devote to becoming an expert in marketing. *Marketing Boot Camp* solves this problem.

The authors, whom I have known for years, comprehend how to take the complexities of running a business and put them into understandable and easy-to-implement, step-by-step strategies.

This handy desk reference makes it easy for you to find what you need to know with a minimum of time and effort. Each success strategy is a "golden nugget" of information that alone can increase your sales and boost your profits. For example, the section on networking starts where many other books stop by showing you where to look, and exactly what to say. In-depth coverage is included in each of the 85 *Marketing Boot Camp* success strategies, offering you the real "how to" of what it takes to make more money with your marketing.

A major benefit of *Marketing Boot Camp* is that each one of the success strategies is based on the authors' actual experience and the successful results they've generated for their clients and themselves. With 30 years combined experience in the trenches, Arnold and Dan provide you with practical skills and not just theory. Their consulting, seminars and training programs have helped thousands from start-ups to those in major corporations successfully develop their businesses for maximum potential.

To be successful today you need the "marketing edge." *Marketing Boot Camp* is one book that will help you stay on top. As the saying goes, "Sew the same seeds and you'll reap the same rewards." In other words, produce the same results that successful people produce and you too will be successful. Follow the guidelines in *Marketing Boot Camp* and you won't go wrong.

> Jeff Davidson
> Author of *Breathing Space, Living and Working at a Comfortable Pace in a Sped-up Society* and *Marketing on a Shoestring*

Preface

"In today's ultra-competitive and mature markets, 'Relationship Marketing' is the new imperative to building and maintaining lasting bonds, customer satisfaction and increased sales."
— THE AUTHORS

Money-making marketing opportunities are staggering for individuals and organizations that know how to build lasting relationships with their target audiences.

Think of your business as a gold mine. Hidden beneath the surface are untapped assets and profits just waiting to be discovered. *The "9/18" Relationship Marketing System* and straight-to-the-point strategies you're about to read will help you unearth the wealth that lies waiting. The goal of this book is simple: **to help you make more money with your marketing by showing you how to build and nurture relationships, get better qualified leads, make more sales, and make more repeat sales at a lower cost.**

Here you'll find the plan, the process and the productivity tools that, when properly applied and sustained, will give you an almost "unfair advantage" over your complacent competitors. The reason? Ninety-five percent of today's businesses cannot or will not market in this systematic, organized, disciplined manner.

One of the ultimate benefits this book offers is the peace of mind you'll enjoy when you can *predictably generate qualified prospects and customers whenever you want them.* Because when *you're* in control of the marketing process, you'll be able to work the same amount of time (or less), make more money, and spend more stress-free time with the people you're *really* doing all of this for . . . your family.

Marketing Boot Camp is written concisely for the busy executive who's constantly on the run and doesn't have a minute to waste. Is this you? Whether yours is a small, mid-sized, or large firm—national, local or regional—the case studies, checklists, guidelines, ideas, action plans, resources and step-by-step strategies will cover your questions and concerns. Many of our readers say they keep *Marketing Boot Camp* on or near their desks as a ready-reference marketing consultant.

We recommend you first become familiar with *The "9/18" Relationship Marketing System* presented in the beginning of the book. After that, you may want skip to the battle-tested tools, techniques and strategies that will personally provide you with the fastest results.

It's been said that experience is a hard teacher. Our purpose for writing this book is to accelerate your marketing success by providing you with "street smart" advice that could otherwise take you years to learn—helpful knowledge offered by two men with over 35 years of combined "in the trenches" marketing experiences.

Marketing is always a work in progress. Some of these strategies will mean quick profits. Others will take you on a slower, yet ultimately prosperous road. There may be no shortcuts to true marketing and monetary success, but there is a faster lane and it's now in your hands.

We salute your impending victories.

—J. Daniel McComas, Arnold Sanow

SECTION 1

Think Like a Marketer

MARKETING BOOT CAMP

Success   #**1**   Strategy

To Make More Money, Make A Difference

"No one can become rich without first enriching others."
— ANDREW CARNEGIE

Why are you in business? What's your first thought? If it's to make money, you're not alone. Invariably, 95% of our workshop attendees unabashedly proclaim their money-making quest when asked this question. Of course, when they say their goal is "to make money" they're right. And so are you. However, this thinking places the proverbial cart before the horse.

Recently, we met with the dean of adult education at a large university to discuss training programs. As we entered his office he said "OK, what are *you guys* selling?" We immediately assured him that we weren't selling anything but were there to discuss his training needs and challenges. Without hesitating he remarked that no salesperson had *ever* said *that* to him before. Instantly, his wall of resistance crumbled and we enjoyed a productive dialog. Our prospective client was highly receptive to our proposed solutions which we believe will result in a mutually profitable partnership. The moral: Don't sell . . . *solve* people's problems.

Lewis Carroll said one of the deep secrets of life is that all that is really worth doing is what we do for others. The key that will unlock the secret to *your* marketing success is this:

> *Take people from where they are to where they want to be and your prosperity will be assured.*

You see, when you consistently help people solve their problems or achieve their desires and dreams, psychic and monetary rewards *will* come your way. It's the ancient "law of reciprocity" and it will never fail you if your initial mission is to help and serve others.

MARKETING BOOT CAMP

Success   #**2**   Strategy

We're *All* In The Business of Marketing

Is your business growing as fast as it should? Are you earning what you're worth? Would you like to skyrocket your income to new heights? Please, listen carefully. *No matter what business you're in, you're in the business of marketing.* Knowledge about your product or service is *worthless* if you don't have a steady stream of interested prospective customers to talk to, or a roster of clients and customers to serve.

Taking the time to learn how to create and keep customers is the most profitable investment you will ever make. Whether you handle the marketing and sales yourself, hire someone to do it, or are an employee responsible for bringing home the bacon, *you* are the ultimate marketing director for your organization.

That means you must invest time and money in your marketing education. The reason is simple: The more you learn, the more you'll earn. Study successful marketers. Soak up information like a sponge. Stay current with newspapers and periodicals like *The Wall Street Journal, Fortune, Entrepreneur, Inc.,* and the resources we recommend throughout this book. Moreover, get your hands on marketing and sales books and magazines, newsletters and audio/video tapes. Also attend seminars where you'll meet valuable contacts and discover new strategies not yet revealed in books.

Marketing can make or break a business. It doesn't matter whether yours is a start-up or service business, a volunteer group, government institution or retail establishment—your lifeblood is customer cultivation and conversion. Thus, you must constantly reevaluate and improve your products and services. Get out of the office, put your ear to the ground and find out what's happening in the ever-changing world of your customers and prospects. Remember, when you give them what they want, they'll give you what you want.

MARKETING BOOT CAMP

Success   #**3**   Strategy

Marketing . . .
Your Golden Key To Success

"True marketing starts out with the customer, his demographics, his realities, his needs, his values. It does not ask, 'What do we want to sell?' It asks, 'What does the consumer want to buy?' . . . The aim of marketing is to make selling superfluous."
— PETER DRUCKER

The most successful companies and individuals are *marketing driven*. Your marketing efforts should have one objective: to open doors for sales people and shorten the selling cycle. Everyday, you must focus on generating and reselling customers. You do this by developing a systematic marketing *process* designed to reach the right people at the right time with the right marketing messages and offers.

Fueling The Buyer's Enthusiasm

Marketing is finding and filling other people's goals, beliefs, wants and choices. In short, helping others get more out of life. It's getting people's attention and making them aware that you have a better solution to an old problem. Or, if you're introducing a new product or service, it's uncovering and solving new problems. It's communicating with and educating potential buyers to get them *predisposed* to purchase what you're offering. It's tipping the scales in your favor by showing people how the benefits of your product or service outweigh its costs. It's also bringing customers through the door in droves and getting significant numbers of phone inquiries and requests for more information from qualified, interested prospects **everyday**!

When you're marketing effectively, sales should be an easier, more natural conclusion to the process of getting your products or services into the hands of your buyers.

Be Pro-Active, Not Re-Active

Marketing is a moving target. With technological advances occurring at breakneck speed, consumers' "wants" can change virtually overnight. That means you must habitually keep your antennae up to exploit timely opportunities. And don't forget to have fun! Successful marketing is a genuine high. There's nothing quite like the thrill of selling a ton of products, landing a new account and helping others improve their lives! If your goal is long-term profitability, you must focus on creating a relationship with your customers based on trust. And relationships are maintained by frequent contact.

SECTION 2

The Marketing System That Builds Relationships And Profits

MARKETING BOOT CAMP

Success #**4** Strategy

Double, Even Triple Your Income In The Next 18 Months With *The "9/18" Relationship Marketing System*

"Little happens in a relationship until the individuals learn to trust each other."— DAVID W. JOHNSON

The "9/18" Relationship Marketing System is the conceptual foundation of this book. The tools, techniques and strategies that follow are integral components you will use to launch and sustain your money-making process. This automated database marketing system relies on personal contacts and multiple mailings (a minimum of 9 in 18 months). It's primary purpose is to build rapport, empathy and **lasting relationships** with your key audiences. With careful planning and commitment it will dramatically increase awareness, acceptance, preference and demand for your products and services. Here's how it works:

1. Establish and maintain a database of your target audiences— prospects, customer/clients, centers of influence, media contacts and suppliers.

2. Reflect an attitude of "giving instead of getting." Every other month over the next 18 months, you'll mail useful information designed to educate, motivate, benefit or reward your target audiences for responding to you. The mailing campaign will be interspersed with personal telephone contacts and face-to-face meetings.

3. As confidence and trust in you grows, watch your leads, sales, repeat sales, media exposure and profits soar!

4. Repeat the cycle with your prime prospects and current customers.

When people have choices, they invariably go where they are made to feel special, important and appreciated.

The most effective strategy we know for leveraging your marketing efforts is to *consistently communicate* customer-centered, customer-caring information and advice that builds trust and confidence in you, your company and your products or services. *The "9/18" Relationship Marketing System* will help you reach this goal efficiently and economically.

One of the costliest marketing and selling mistakes we can make is to "ask for the order" before we know our prospects' wants and needs. This ill-fated strategy, says Steven Covey *(The 7 Habits of Highly Effective People),* is "attempting to make a withdrawal before you've made any deposits."

Picture this. You've just made a sales "cold call" and somehow manage to get past the "gatekeeper" secretary. You shuffle into your prospect's office and there staring you down is an irritated-looking manager. You introduce yourself and your company but before you can say another word he growls:

> *I don't know who you are.*
> *I don't know your company.*
> *I don't know your company's product or service.*
> *I don't know what your company stands for.*
> *I don't know your company's customers.*
> *I don't know your company's record.*
> *I don't know your company's reputation.*
> *Now—what was it you wanted to sell me?*

Ouch! The moral: the sale starts l-o-n-g before the salesperson calls. For years McGraw Hill has successfully used this strategy to sell ad space in its business publications. This strategy sums up the crucial need for building **relationships** with your prospects, customers/clients, suppliers, the media and, in some cases, your competitors!

You see, *consistent contact* with your targeted groups maximizes your marketing effectiveness for several reasons. First, research shows that confidence and familiarity are primary factors in someone's decision to buy what you're selling—or to refer you to someone else. The other sales motivators in order of importance are quality, selection, service and price. Obviously, price moves up this scale if you've positioned yourself as a low-cost or discount provider.

Clockwork Communication Yields Profitable Results

Repetition works. Persistence pays. A study published in *New Equipment Digest Magazine* shows that 63% of the prospects who asked for information about a product took three months or longer to buy. And nearly 20% took over a year. Additionally, most sales fail simply because a marketer gives up too soon. In fact, several studies have shown that 80% of all sales close between the fifth and ninth contacts! Billionaire businessman H. Ross Perot says "most people give up just when they're about to achieve success. They quit on the one yard line in the last minute of the game, one foot from a winning touchdown."

In many cases "the last one seen is the first one called." *The "9/18" Relationship Marketing System* helps you create *top-of-mind awareness* so you'll be the undisputed provider of choice when your prospects are ready to buy and your customers are ready to buy again. Here's the good news for you. Most businesses will *never* approach their marketing in this organized and disciplined manner. One excuse you'll hear is that they're too busy to market. Yet when the work slows, you'll find them scrambling to fill the new business void. Is this a familiar marketing malady in your business? If so, we suggest you adopt and communicate with your target audience at least 9 times over the next 18 months to keep the phone ringing, the orders and leads coming in, and ready-to-buy prospects and customers walking into your office or store. Yes, this system requires patience and persistence, but it *will* yield profitable results when properly applied and sustained. You see, in many cases a "no" now means "give me more time." Thus, you must stay connected with your buyers and potential buyers through personal contacts and benefit-rich marketing communications materials that get the *right information* into the *right hands* at the *right time* to make them say YES!

We know what you're thinking: "I get so much junk mail, and so do my prospects and customers. Aren't my materials going to get trashed immediately?" The answer in the majority of instances is a resounding NO! if you are vigilant about communicating information that offers value, news and helpful advice.

Results-Driven Marketing Tools And Techniques

Here is an arsenal of marketing weapons you can use to create an ongoing marketing communications *system* to build trust and generate more leads, sales and repeat sales. Many of these tools and techniques are interactive direct response vehicles designed to open a dialog and elicit a reply with your target audience. Several of these methods will help you sell your products or services immediately, while others will take more time:

- ➪ Use two-step "pre-heat letters" to warm up prospects.
- ➪ Send lead-generating and sales-closing letters.
- ➪ Send serial sales letters—a sequence of 3–12 personal, nurturing letters to "grow" winning relationships.
- ➪ Use direct mail packages.
- ➪ Use telemarketing to generate leads, set appointments and close sales.
- ➪ Buy classified and small space ads in select business or consumer publications.
- ➪ Mail general articles of interest to your prospects and customers.
- ➪ Use articles written by you and published in a newspaper, industry newsletter or trade publication. Article reprints are excellent sales tools.
- ➪ Join chambers, associations and networking groups and attend (really attend!) the meetings.
- ➪ Send news releases to the media *and* to your prospects and customers.
- ➪ Sponsor an open house mixer or mini-seminar at your office for your best clients and prospects.

↪ Offer a free seminar and create a news release to announce it. Remember to invite the media. Later, send a "seminar high-lights" report to non-attendees and invite them to call you with any questions about the material you covered.

↪ Teach an adult education class and inform your target audience and the media via news release.

↪ Mail a "needs assessment survey" for pro-active customer relations or to survey prospects.

↪ Write case studies of problems you've solved or opportunities you've created for your clients and mail to your prospects and the media.

↪ Create print, audio and video brochures, sell sheets and flyers.

↪ Use Q & A formats to answer typical questions or objections your target audience consistently raises.

↪ Buy yellow pages ads.

↪ Use radio and televisional commercials.

↪ Use television "infomercials."

↪ Send postcards.

↪ Send post-purchase communications—alert customers to new products and services.

↪ Be remembered by giving your customers ad specialties/imprinted promotional products.

↪ Send thank you cards and letters for customer purchases and referrals.

↪ Send seasonal greeting cards and gift.

For the record, *The "9/18" Relationship Marketing System* helped Dan personally sell over $1 million of business for a small ad agency in less than 18 months and currently keeps prospective clients consistently calling *him* for business. And staying "close to the customer" through this systematic marketing process has allowed Arnold to build an incredible referral network that helps him book over 130 paid speaking engagements every year!

Now it's *your* turn to tap into this money-making relationship-building system.

MARKETING BOOT CAMP

Success   #**5**   Strategy

Unlock The Power Of Your PC
To Win More Customers

People buy from people who take the time to thoroughly understand their needs. That is, marketers who consistently demonstrate—through actions—a long-term commitment to an ongoing, mutually beneficial and interactive relationship.

Effective use of *marketing and sales automation* will help you build and nurture winning relationships and sales more economically. According to the *Harvard Business Review,* if marketing and sales average 15% to 35% of total corporate costs, using automation tools to achieve a 20% reduction in sales expenses can add 3% to 7% to your company's bottom line. Additionally, sales increases arising from advanced marketing and sales automation range from 10% to more than 30% with investment returns often exceeding 100%.

The engine that drives *The "9/18" Relationship Marketing System* is your database marketing. Whether you use off-the-shelf packages or a customized system, marketing and sales automation will help you:

- ➪ Connect with more potential customers more often
- ➪ Increase your closing percentage and repeat business
- ➪ Minimize customer defections
- ➪ Initiate customer reactivation programs
- ➪ Identify which marketing efforts are producing
- ➪ Be alert to cross-selling potential within companies
- ➪ Identify customers with a high propensity to buy additional products/services
- ➪ Expedite order entry procedures and service requests
- ➪ Remember appropriate "call back" dates and times

↪ Produce instantaneous reports from the field

↪ Solve customer problems faster

↪ Reduce paperwork

↪ Respond quickly to changing market opportunities

Sending a continuing series of sales letters, newsletters, postcards, etc., can be a tedious process. Fortunately, there are several "Relationship Manager" software programs designed to automate the process. Rich Bohn, nationally acclaimed publisher and sales automation specialist, makes his living by pushing, prodding and educating sales professionals and small-business owners to leverage their marketing mailings and sales calls using automation software. Rich recommends the following software to help you design and implement multi-step, time-sequenced mailings, telephone calls and personal sales calls: *Strategic Results* (currently $499.95 for your IBM compatible PC from Perceptive Solutions, Inc., P.O. Box 12956, Lake Park, FL 33403-0956, (407) 626-4561) and *Market Master*, a Macintosh-based program (currently $395 from Breakthrough Productions, 210 Park Avenue, Nevada City, CA 95959, (916) 265-0911).

And if you're looking for "state-of-the-moment tips" for using computer automation to market and sell more, ask Rich about his *Sales Automation Survival Guide*. You can contact him at The Denali Group, 2815 NW Pine Cone Drive, Issaquah, WA 98027-8698, (206) 392-3514.

Caution: Of course you can't rely on technology alone. Relationship building is a *people function* that requires your personal touch. If that means calling someone Bill instead of William or Sandi instead of Sandra in your letter salutations, by all means do it!

Note: If you don't yet work with computers (for heaven's sake, please learn how to use this technology!) or find you don't have the time to input names, generate labels or consistently handle this kind of methodical marketing process in-house, consider working with a marketing consultant or mail house. Look under "Mail House" or "Letter Shop" in your phone book or in your Chamber of Commerce directory.

SECTION 3

Tools, Techniques & Strategies To Grow Your Business

MARKETING BOOT CAMP

Success   #**6**   Strategy

Deploy Direct Response Marketing For Faster Results

General advertising is designed primarily to generate attention. Unless you have a big bucks budget, this type of advertising will quickly sink your business.

Your marketing needs to pay its own way. That's why the majority of marketing materials we advocate in *The "9/18" Relationship Marketing System* are **direct response** tools. That is, they ask people to **respond to you** by picking up the phone, mailing back a reply card, placing an order or visiting your store. Asking people to *do something* leverages your marketing dollars.

Give Your Prospects A REASON To Connect With You

Direct response marketing maximizes your pulling power. It is designed to help you generate new leads and sales, donations, acquire volunteers, sign-up members, eliminate the high cost of a sales staff, open new markets and romance current customers. It also helps you test the effectiveness of your marketing messages because the responses mean the results are immediate.

Avoid Lifeless, Boring And Ineffective Institutional Marketing

How many ads have you seen that brag about the advertiser and nothing about how it can help potential consumers? Business card ads are a prime (yawn) example of this. Institutional or "image" ads are typically "me-centered" monologues instead of customer-focused dialogs and must be jettisoned from your marketing methods . . . now! Please . . . tell people how you can improve their lives and get them to connect with you.

MARKETING BOOT CAMP

Success   #**7**   Strategy

Educate Your Way To Greater Profits

Knowledge is power . . . but it's also *profits!* Here's why educating your customers and prospects on the **advantages** you offer will give you a decided marketing edge.

Buyers simply have a mind-boggling array of choices today and find it difficult to differentiate between the profusion of parity products and services. They're more savvy. And more persnickety. Additionally, you must overcome people's natural inclination to be skeptical or apathetic toward your business. Education breaks down the wall of consumer resistance by building credibility and confidence in the minds of your readers, listeners and viewers.

When you're marketing properly, you won't be guilty of bragging about yourself. Why? Because you'll benefit from the *perceived* ability to solve a problem, increase productivity, decrease costs, save time or find new solutions to old customer problems. The key to a successful customer education campaign is to *consistently communicate* useful information to help your target audience understand your problem-solving advantages.

There's an equally important reason for educating your prospects and customers. Effective education-based marketing gives compelling, irresistible "reasons why" your product or service is superior and indispensable to the lives of your customers. It provides specific evidence of the emotional advantages you've promised and the logical reasons for buying.

To gain and retain business, you'll need to maintain an ongoing educational exchange with your database of customers, prospects and suppliers. Yes, it takes more time, effort and patience, but seminars, newsletters, "reasons why" sales letters, Q & A sheets, "advertorial" ads and case studies are powerful and profitable tools that position you or your company as the leading authority in your field. And people buy from individuals and companies they know and trust.

MARKETING BOOT CAMP

Success   #**8**   Strategy

Know *Why* People Buy And Watch Your Sales Soar

By understanding the steps people take when deciding to buy a product or service, you'll know the right marketing strategy to use and when to use it. The four stages people go through are:

1. **Information Search**—Remember the old saying, "Don't judge a book by its cover"? Unfortunately, that's what everybody does. In this first step people *will* judge you by your printed materials, your dress, your mannerisms, your advertising, business cards and other information about your business.
2. **Evaluation Behavior**—In the second step they will compare you with your competitors or what they perceive as a good service or product. They will consider the pro's and con's and the benefits you offer.
3. **Purchase Decision**—This is when they make the crucial decision to buy your product or service and is usually based on your Unique Selling Position (USP) or the unique benefit or advantage that separates you from everyone else.
4. **Post-Purchase Feelings.** What you do after the sale is the key for future success. People will either get what they expected, not get what they expected or get much more than they expected. Give them more than they expect and your referrals will skyrocket!

MARKETING BOOT CAMP

Success   #**9**   Strategy

Would You Buy From You? . . . A Self Test

The Greek teacher and philosopher Plato wrote: "The life that is unexamined is not worth living."

The English essayist and historian Thomas Carlyle said: "What we have done is the only mirror by which we can see what we are."

One of the most effective ways to assess your effectiveness in handling customers is via the question: "If you were the customer, would you buy from yourself?" You would if you scored well on the following quiz. Answer each question by checking the appropriate YES or NO blank.

	YES	NO
1. Is your image one of honest and straightforward sincerity?	_____	_____
2. Based on your experience with customers over the past year or so, *from the buyer's point of view,* would you be classified as reliable?	_____	_____
3. Could you say your customers obtained special benefits dealing with you they wouldn't have obtained from others?	_____	_____
4. Do you think you come off as an expert in the eyes of your customers?	_____	_____
5. Have you been effective helping to solve customer problems?	_____	_____
6. Wherever possible, would you say you handled customer complaints to the buyer's satisfaction?	_____	_____
7. Is **integrity** one of the most important words in your vocabulary?	_____	_____
8. Apart from your business dealings, do you think customers believe you have their personal welfare and well-being at heart?	_____	_____
9. Can you honestly say most of your company's customers think of you as a friend as well as business associate?	_____	_____
10. Do customers look upon you as a good reliable source of product and industry information?	_____	_____
11. Has doing business with you contributed positively to most of your customers' profit performance?	_____	_____
12. Would most of your company's customers continue dealing with you even if a competitor approached them with a price that's a little bit lower?	_____	_____

Total No. of YES Answers _____

MARKETING BOOT CAMP

Success   #**10**   Strategy

Discover Your Customers' Wants Through Low-Cost Market Research

Ask

Always ask clients during and after the service to check out their satisfaction level. The CEO at Virgin Air talks with customers on at least one flight a month; 6 Flags Over Georgia asks 50 customers their opinions of the park everyday.

Observe

See how clients use your products or services. Look at their body language. Are they happy?

User Groups

Organize a user group of customers to meet on a regular basis to provide you with feedback on how well you're doing.

Hire a Mystery Shopper

Hire someone to use your service or buy your product. This should be done without the knowledge of your staff. The mystery shopper reports on the transaction from start to finish.

Focus Groups

This is where you get 8 to 12 people together for two-hour sessions to find out their attitudes and beliefs about your products or services. The objective of focus groups made up of clients is to find what you must do to get more clients like them. Another purpose for focus groups is to gain valuable feedback on new products and services from a mixture of prospective and current clients.

Secondary Information

This is information that is already available. You can find information about your type of business through past issues of newspapers and trade magazines at the library. Computers can easily scan the information you want.

MARKETING BOOT CAMP

Success   #**11**   Strategy

Follow The Trends To Exploit Opportunities

No marketing program is complete without your understanding and being aware of trends. Trends help you determine the viability of a product or service as well as knowing how and whom to market to. You can find out how to capitalize on the newest trends in trade publications that relate to your business through associations connected with your industry (an excellent resource is *Gayle's Encyclopedia of Associations*), through the *Kiplinger Report* (published by *Changing Times Magazine*) and through general information located in media publications such as *The Wall Street Journal, Time Magazine, Newsweek, Entrepreneur, Inc. Magazine, Business Week* and others.

Some general trends for the '90s and beyond that were compiled by *Business Week* and Link Resources, Inc., include:

⇨ Advances in business technology and communications will allow small businesses to compete with large companies in the years ahead.

⇨ The number of Americans over 65 will continue to grow rapidly through the 1990s. By 2020, one in six Americans will be over 65, and many will opt to stay in the work force rather than retire.

⇨ Men and women over 55 control over 50% of the discretionary income.

⇨ In 1950 there were an average of 93,000 businesses started. Now there are over 600,000 businesses started each year.

⇨ The home labor force has been expanding by 7% to 9% a year. At this point over 31 million people work from home. (This number combines people in their own business and companies that allow employees to work from home.)

⇨ Recent immigrants will play an increasing role in America's business development through the 1990s, a reality borne out by statistics. By the year 2015, for example, the Hispanic population will make up the largest minority segment in the nation.

⇨ Flextime, satellite work stations and other innovative working arrangements will allow employees of larger companies to increase overall quality of life. While more time will be spent at home with family, more time will also be spent at home working.

⇨ The environment, a major area of concern, will take center stage in government and business. Companies will be expected to demonstrate an interest in protecting the environment through their activities and new products.

You must constantly stay on top of "crest of the wave" trends and emerging technologies to exploit opportunities. Dedicate yourself to following new marketing techniques, new inventions, new industries, new technologies, societal changes and more to better serve your customers' ever-shifting wants and needs.

Another excellent resource to chart the future's impact on your business is *The Popcorn Report* by Faith Popcorn (Harper Business), which is available in most bookstores.

MARKETING BOOT CAMP

Success   #**12**   Strategy

Know Yourself and Your Customers . . . Your Marketing Audit

Before investing time and money into various marketing strategies, it's essential to complete a *marketing audit* to better understand yourself and your customers. Too many times we make arbitrary decisions without any solid marketing information. The results can be disastrous. To enhance your marketing prowess, answer the following questions:

1. **What Business Am I *Really* In?** The first question you must answer is, What client needs does my business meet? For example, a shopping center is really in the entertainment and recreation business and is competing against other recreational and entertainment activities. By realizing this, your marketing strategy will focus on your true competition.

2. **Where Can I Diversify?** Whether you're just starting a business or have been in business a long time, you need to consider additional services you can offer your customers. For example, one computer consulting and sales firm we worked with bought and sold used computers. Companies would come in and buy hundreds of these computers at one time. But they also needed services such as training, maintenance, consulting and software. By offering its customers these add-on services directly and through subcontractors, the computer company's sales skyrocketed!

3. **What Is the Perceived Quality of the Service or Merchandise I Sell?** People buy for their reasons, not ours. Although we may feel that we have a high-quality product or service, the customer is the one who really defines quality. For example, a while ago an inventor built a mousetrap. In his mind this was the high-

est quality mousetrap in the world. It was indestructible because it was made of metal designed to last 20 years. He thought he had an instant top seller. Unfortunately, sales were very poor. When potential customers were asked why they didn't buy it, they said they didn't want a mousetrap that would last for 20 years, but one they could throw out with the mouse! So, when thinking about quality remember the saying, "To Sell Jack Jones What Jack Jones Buys, You Need to See Jack Jones Through Jack Jones' Eyes." The feast is determined by the consumer, not the chef.

4. **What Kind of Image Do I Want to Project?** One of the keys to offering a successful product or service is to *position* it in the mind of the customer. The marketing term *positioning* means how you want your product or service to be seen in the eyes of the consumer. For example, one major soft drink company did a survey and found that 13% of the American public drinks sodas for breakfast. To position its soda as a breakfast drink, the company redesigned the can with a picture of the sun rising and a rooster crowing and sold it in the breakfast drink section.

5. **How Do I Compare With the Competition?** There are three reasons why you need to know about your competition. The first is to determine where you have the advantages, the second reason is to know why and how they are better, and the third reason is to copy success. Tony Robbins in his book *Unlimited Power* states, "Sew the Same Seeds and You'll Reap the Same Rewards." In other words, produce the same results that successful people produce and you too will be successful. Some of the areas where you need to compare yourself with the competition are Product, Price, Promotion, Place, Package and Personnel.

6. **What Benefits Do I Offer My Customers?** In other words, what can your client save, gain, accomplish or avoid by using your product or service?

7. **Who Are My Customers?** There is no issue more important to you than knowing your customers. Most people try to be everything to everyone. This dilutes our marketing messages as well as our time and money. We need to focus on the 20% of the cus-

tomers that will give us 80% of our income. Characteristics we may want to focus on include, age, income, geographic region, lifestyle, attitudes, usage patterns and more.

8. **Can They Afford Our Product or Service?** Do you have different services and products available to meet the needs of your various market segments, with prices they can afford?

9. **When Do They Buy Your Product or Services?** By understanding the key buying times of the year, you'll know the best times to market your product or service.

10. **Why Do They Buy From Me?** There is one main reason why people buy your product or service. You must be unique or different. This is known as your *Unique Selling Position (USP)*. Uniqueness could be as simple as being available to consult with clients late at night or perhaps a dentist who offers the use of his fax machine and telephone while a patient is waiting for an appointment.

14 Easy Ways To Learn What You Need To Know About Your Competitors

Follow these guidelines for competitive intelligence gathering. Learn the following information from public sources: 1) Who are your competitors? 2) What services do your competitors offer? 3) When did your competitors go into business? 4) Where do your competitors plan to expand? 5) Why are your competitors successful or unsuccessful? 6) How big are your competitors operations? AND MORE . . .

State Government

➪ Contact your State Department of Commerce for the Articles of Incorporation of your competitors.

➪ Contact your Contract Administration Office for contracts awarded to your competitor.

⇨ Contact your State Securities Office for financial information and stock offerings by your competitor.

⇨ Contact your State Licensing Office for professional or occupational permits or licenses granted to your competitor.

⇨ Contact your State Attorney General's Office for investigations being conducted about your competitor.

Local Government

⇨ Contact your Business or Economic Development Office staff, Small Business Development Centers and Chamber of Commerce to learn an insider's knowledge about your competitor.

⇨ Contact your Property Appraiser and/or Tax Assessor to learn important details about your competitor's facilities.

⇨ Contact your Clerks Office to learn about your competitor's real estate activity.

⇨ Contact your Building Department and or Planning Department to learn about your competitor's facility expansion plans.

⇨ Contact your Consumer Protection Office to learn about complaints or investigations filed against your competitor.

⇨ Contact your library to review clipping files, reference sources including Dun & Bradstreet and Ward's Business Directory Listings.

Other Sources

⇨ For general information contact the business reporter or editor of your local newspaper, who covers your industry.

⇨ Contact local trade associations.

⇨ Contact companies in related industries.

Source: Linda E. Gelfin, Principal of L. Gelfin Associates, a consulting firm specializing in business research and information resources, located in Silver Spring, Maryland.

MARKETING BOOT CAMP

Success   #**13**   Strategy

The Marketing Plan . . .
Your Blueprint For Success

A person or a business without a plan is like a ship without a rudder; which-
ever way the wind blows is the way you'll go. You'll end up somewhere,
but it may not be where you want to be. To realistically reach the goals
you've set, you need to have a *written* strategic marketing plan. The following is the step-by-step process we go through when developing a marketing plan for our clients and one you can use to develop your own profitable marketing strategy.

Marketing is a process and, as such, it never ends. Once the information is compiled and the plan designed, it has to be refined and re-
vamped to accommodate changes in the marketplace.

The subsequent steps are to be answered by you and your staff, but
the importance of market research is always stressed. After all, the goal
of marketing is to make people want to do business with you. And it's
impossible to develop a consumer orientation unless you know your prospects and clients and their needs.

Make sure anyone affected by the plan is included in its development.
When working with our clients, we usually go offsite to a hotel or home
and spend several days discussing and answering the following questions:

1. **What business are you in?** The best run companies have mission statements. They are used to establish a direction and focus
   . . . and are extremely important. Mission statements help you,
   your associates and customers know exactly what you do. They
   also provide direction for routine activities and innovation. For
   example, The Business Source's mission statement and reason
   for being is, "The Business Source is a 'one stop' business devel-

opment and training firm. We offer seminars, workshops and training in Customer Service, Marketing, Business Development, Entrepreneurship, Presentation and Communication Skills. In addition, we consult with start-ups to growth companies to perform market research, business and marketing plans, marketing and business consulting, and personalized coaching/mentoring."

In a short paragraph, write out your company's mission:

_____

_____

_____

_____

2. **What strengths do you have in the marketplace that people know about?** Every company has strengths and you are ultimately judged by the people with whom and for whom you do business. If you asked your clients to list your strengths, what would they write? (Please realize the importance of market research in coming up with these answers.)

_____

_____

_____

_____

3. **What weaknesses do you have in the marketplace that people know about?** All companies have weaknesses. And, like strengths, they are used by your clients to judge your company. In the minds of the people you serve, what are your company's weaknesses?

_____

_____

_____

_____

4. **What strengths do you have that are not known in the marketplace?** All companies have strengths which aren't known or appreciated by those outside of your company. These factors can influence the direction of the marketing plan. For example, you or your staff may have taken the latest state-of-the-art training programs. This strength can be used to reinforce your marketing efforts because it provides an opportunity to "advertise" the dedication and expertise of your staff.

_____

_____

_____

_____

5. **What weaknesses do you have that are not known in the marketplace?** Your company may have weaknesses which are not generally known by outsiders. For example, poor communication may be a problem. While this may be an internal weakness, it won't be long before it becomes apparent to people outside of your business.

_____

_____

_____

_____

6. **What are the opportunities and threats that relate to your business?** Opportunities and threats are things that you can't control. For example, an opportunity may be that certain new government regulations require insurance agents to take a special kind of training. This may be an opening for your business to provide an educational program that fills this need. On the other hand, a threat could be that certain new government taxes may

cripple your business. By knowing and anticipating various opportunities and threats we can determine multiple ways to handle
them.

_____

_____

_____

_____

7. **What do you have that's marketable?** To be successful we need
   to focus on the products and services that produce the greatest
   benefit for us. A rule known as the "Paretto Principle" states that
   20% of the products or services we sell produce 80% of our income.
   Therefore, we need to list in order the products and services that
   produce the greatest benefit.

_____

_____

_____

_____

8. **Targeting.** Reflect on your marketable assets and goals. Then
   ask who is or might be most interested. For a marketing plan to
   be effective, the targets must be clearly identified. These are the
   people to whom you will direct your communication efforts. Of
   all the people served by your company—internally (employees)
   and externally—which ones will be the primary targets?

   Internally:

_____

_____

_____

_____

Externally:

_____

_____

_____

_____

9. **Establish goals.** Goals are established to capitalize on strengths and to minimize or eliminate weaknesses. They are the road maps to a more effective company. For example, if customer service is a weakness then one of your goals may be, "Develop a customer service program to reduce complaints 20% by next June."

   Considering your company's strengths, weaknesses, opportunities, threats, marketable assets and mission, list the goals that relate to your company:

_____

_____

_____

_____

10. **Goals are nice, but . . .** Goals provide focus, but the keys to success are the action steps (objectives) to reach the goals you have set. Good objectives tell how a goal will be addressed. They are specific and measurable. Based on your goals, what are some of the action steps you'll take?

    Goal One: _____

    Action Step 1 _____

    Action Step 2 _____

    Action Step 3 _____

Goal Two: _____

Action Step 1 _____

Action Step 2 _____

Action Step 3 _____

Goal Three: _____

Action Step 1 _____

Action Step 2 _____

Action Step 3 _____

11. **Putting it together.** On the following page is a planning work-sheet we use with our clients to help them prepare their "road map." It includes:

    The goal—The goal needs to be specific, measurable and acceptable to all involved. It must be realistic and have a time frame. For example, "We want to send out 5,000 direct mail pieces every month and get a 2% response starting in June of this year and ending in June of next year."

    Action Steps—These are the step-by-step strategies we need to accomplish to reach our goal.

    Resource Requirements—This consists of the money, material, time and space needed for each action step.

    Coordination—Who in the organization will be the coordinator?

    Time Frame—Deadlines, due dates and time frames should all be listed here.

    Evaluation—What were the results of each step?

12. **Focus.** While working on the plan, keep focused on the channels of communication (how people find out about you), the competition and how you're positioned in the marketplace.

Far too much marketing produces mediocre results because business people refuse to invest the up-front time researching their marketing environment, setting the proper objectives and evaluating the results as they go along. Please don't be one of them.

Planning Worksheet

Goal:

Action Step	Specific Steps and Resource Requirements (people, money, material, space)	Coordination Requirements	Target Dates Begin	End	Eval.

MARKETING BOOT CAMP

Success **#14** Strategy

What's This Gonna Cost Me? Your Marketing Investment

The answer is . . . that depends. Marketing budgets are as individual as fingerprints. Your budget will be contingent upon many factors including: how long you've been in business; the percentage of the market you're seeking (do you want to be the dominant company or can you be profitable with a smaller share?); your competitive situation; your hottest selling months; timely, yet unforeseen opportunities your business can exploit; and so on.

The primary goal of this book is to show you how to maximize your marketing efforts by creating a relationship-based marketing system that **gets results!** Obviously, if you can invest more time (in publicity-generating activities, for example) you'll save on marketing. And, if you can create your marketing documents in-house, you'll save money. One guideline to consider is to base your budget on a percentage of your past annual or anticipated annual sales. The *Advertising To Sales Ratios* chart may prove helpful for the advertising component of your marketing communications budget. However, to stay focused on the future and to help you *act* instead of *react* to marketing opportunities and challenges, you should consider investing between 10% to 15% of your *projected* sales on marketing activities.

Advertising To Sales Ratios For the 200 Largest Ad Spending Industries

Industry	SIC No.	Ad $ as % Sales	Ad $ as % Margin	Annual Ad Growth Rate %
Adhesives and Sealants	2891	2.7	5.6	9.1
Advertising Agencies	7311	2.1	2.4	15.6
Agriculture Chemicals	2870	1.5	7.5	−6.9
Agriculture Production—Crops	100	2.3	8.7	−3.0
Air Cond, Heating, Refrig EQ	3585	1.5	6.1	3.1
Air Courier Services	4513	1.6	14.1	7.2
Air Transport, Scheduled	4512	1.7	58.8	3.9
Apparel & Other Finished Pds	2300	5.1	14.3	9.2
Apparel and Accessory Stores	5600	2.4	6.1	10.4
Auto and Home Supply Stores	5531	1.4	4.7	5.7
Auto Rent & Lease, No Drivers	7510	2.2	3.3	1.7
Bakery Products	2050	10.5	25.0	−4.3
Beverages	2080	8.2	13.8	9.1
Biological Pds, Ex Diagnostics	2836	1.0	3.6	17.5
Bituminous Coal, Lignite Mng	1220	2.0	4.3	6.7
Blankbooks, Binders, Bookbind	2780	2.2	4.2	7.9
Bldg Matl, Hardwr, Garden—Retl	5200	2.2	3.0	−20.7
Books: Pubg, Pubg & Printing	2731	3.4	6.2	5.2
Brdwoven Fabric Mill, Cotton	2211	4.0	16.6	7.3
Brdwovn Fabric Man Made, Silk	2221	2.6	7.4	−55.9
Btld & Can Soft Drinks, Water	2086	4.0	8.8	11.9
Cable and Other Pay TV Svcs	4841	1.3	2.0	−2.5
Calculate, Acct Mach, Ex Comp	3578	1.8	3.7	−2.5
Can Fruit, Veg, Presrv, Jam, Jel	2033	1.5	5.9	−7.9
Can, Froznpresrv Fruit & Veg	2030	7.6	20.1	7.6
Catalog, Mail-Order Houses	5961	6.5	17.6	9.7
Chemicals & Allied Pds—Whsl	5160	1.1	4.0	9.6
Chemicals & Allied Prods	2800	3.6	8.6	2.3
Cigarettes	2111	4.1	6.2	3.3
Cmp and Cmp Software Stores	5734	1.1	13.0	16.6
Cmp Integrated Sys Design	7373	1.3	3.8	0.4
Cmp Processing, Data Prep Svc	7374	1.4	3.1	−5.3
Communications Equip, Nec	3669	2.5	5.5	1.3
Computer & Office Equipment	3570	1.4	3.2	3.7
Computer Communication Equip	3576	1.8	3.1	12.4

Industry	SIC No.	Ad $ as % Sales	Ad $ as % Margin	Annual Ad Growth Rate %
Computer Peripheral Eq, Nec	3577	2.7	5.9	12.1
Computer Storage Devices	3572	1.2	4.9	8.2
Computers & Software—Whsl	5045	1.0	9.9	16.9
Construction Machinery & Eq	3531	0.3	1.0	−4.6
Convrt Papr, Paprbrd, Ex Boxes	2670	2.2	5.1	3.0
Cutlery, Hand Tools, Gen Hrdwr	3420	10.3	19.6	6.9
Dairy Products	2020	1.5	5.8	4.1
Department Stores	5311	2.5	11.1	3.4
Dolls and Stuffed Toys	3942	16.5	30.3	10.6
Drug & Proprietary Stores	5912	1.5	5.4	4.6
Eating Places	5812	3.4	17.0	6.0
Educational Services	8200	7.4	17.6	5.6
Elec Apparatus & Equip—Whsl	5063	14.0	56.6	−3.0
Elec Meas & Test Instruments	3825	2.6	5.2	0.0
Electr, Oth Elec Eq, Ex Cmp	3600	2.8	9.2	10.6
Electric Housewares and Fans	3634	5.8	18.1	2.7
Electric Lighting, Wiring Eq	3640	2.5	8.1	0.9
Electromedical Apparatus	3845	1.1	1.8	7.4
Electronic Components, Nec	3679	0.9	2.8	8.3
Electronic Computers	3571	2.9	7.3	−0.3
Electronic Connectors	3678	3.9	9.4	6.0
Electronic Parts, Eq—Whsl, Nec	5065	2.5	10.4	7.8
Engines and Turbines	3510	2.0	8.3	−15.2
Engr, Acc, Resh, Mgmt, Rel Svcs	8700	0.7	2.9	1.8
Equip Rental & Leasing, Nec	7359	0.7	2.8	1.7
Fabricated Rubber Pds, Nec	3060	0.4	2.7	8.1
Family Clothing Stores	5651	2.4	7.3	9.5
Farm Machinery and Equipment	3523	0.9	4.0	0.5
Finance—Services	6199	0.8	9.0	−2.9
Food and Kindred Products	2000	5.1	15.5	7.5
Footwear, Except Rubber	3140	3.7	9.6	4.6
Functions Rel To Dep Bke, Nec	6099	9.1	58.7	6.6
Furniture Stores	5712	6.5	13.5	6.6
Games, Toys, Chld Veh, Ex Dolls	3944	13.3	24.6	13.9
Gen Med & Surgical Hospitals	8062	1.1	6.1	3.3
General Indl Mach & Eq, Nec	3569	0.5	1.5	−0.7
General Industrial Mach & Eq	3560	2.0	6.7	0.3

Industry	SIC No.	Ad $ as % Sales	Ad $ as % Margin	Annual Ad Growth Rate %
Glass, Glasswr-Pressed, Blown	3220	1.2	2.8	–1.4
Grain Mill Products	2040	8.5	16.7	5.0
Greeting Cards	2771	2.7	4.2	4.8
Groceries & Related Pds—Whsl	5140	1.1	8.1	1.8
Grocery Stores	5411	1.2	5.0	3.2
Gskets, Hose, Bltng-Rubr, Plstc	3050	1.2	3.6	5.5
Hardwr, Plumb, Heat Eq—Whsl	5070	4.7	46.1	1.8
Help Supply Services	7363	1.2	7.0	–3.4
Hobby, Toy, and Game Shops	5945	1.3	4.1	7.2
Home Furniture & Equip Store	5700	3.0	8.7	5.9
Home Health Care Services	8082	0.8	1.7	14.6
Hospital & Medical Svc Plans	6324	1.1	5.0	22.9
Hospitals	8060	4.5	21.7	–0.4
Hotels, Motels, Tourist Courts	7011	3.5	12.5	–1.3
Household Appliances	3630	2.9	9.0	7.4
Household Audio & Video Eq	3651	3.7	11.6	9.5
Household Furniture	2510	4.5	14.5	2.7
Ice Cream & Frozen Desserts	2024	3.7	12.7	2.4
In Vitro, In Vivo Diagnostics	2835	3.3	8.1	18.0
Indl Trucks, Tractors, Trailers	3537	1.1	4.8	4.8
Industrial Measurement Instr	3823	1.1	2.9	0.6
Industrial Organic Chemicals	2860	1.0	3.5	–1.2
Investment Advice	6282	8.0	19.2	12.4
Jewelry Stores	5944	5.1	62.6	12.0
Jewelry, Precious Metal	3911	3.6	9.5	1.4
Knit Outerwear Mills	2253	2.2	6.5	14.6
Knitting Mills	2250	2.4	6.9	7.4
Lab Analytical Instruments	3826	2.1	3.7	7.7
Lawn, Garden Tractors, Equip	3524	1.2	4.3	1.8
Lumber & Oth Bldg Matl—Retl	5211	1.2	4.7	4.8
Machine Tools, Metal Cutting	3541	1.6	4.9	–0.2
Magnetic, Optic Recordng Media	3695	2.9	7.5	9.1
Malt Beverages	2082	5.6	16.7	2.1
Management Services	8741	1.4	6.8	18.9
Meas & Controlling Dev, Nec	3829	1.2	3.3	6.4
Meat Packing Plants	2011	5.3	21.9	6.3

Industry	SIC No.	Ad $ as % Sales	Ad $ as % Margin	Annual Ad Growth Rate %
Medical Laboratories	8071	1.3	3.1	11.5
Men, Yth, Boys Frnsh, Wrk Clthg	2320	3.3	9.3	11.4
Metal Forgings and Stampings	3460	3.7	12.1	12.3
Metalworking Machinery & Eq	3540	3.1	8.3	1.0
Millwork, Veneer, Plywood	2430	1.5	6.8	0.3
Misc Amusement & Rec Service	7990	7.1	21.3	9.7
Misc Business Services	7380	2.0	3.5	12.0
Misc Chemical Products	2890	4.6	10.6	5.1
Misc Elec Machy, Eq, Supplies	3690	3.1	5.7	7.3
Misc Fabricated Metal Prods	3490	0.7	2.4	−10.2
Misc Food Preps, Kindred Pds	2090	2.4	6.0	3.5
Misc General Mdse Stores	5399	4.1	17.8	2.6
Misc Indl, Coml, Machy & Eq	3590	1.9	5.5	7.6
Misc Manufacturng Industries	3990	2.8	6.4	10.6
Misc Nondurable Goods—Whsl	5190	2.2	7.4	18.2
Misc Shopping Goods Stores	5940	4.1	10.8	3.7
Misc Transportation Equip	3790	5.9	23.0	5.0
Miscellaneous Retail	5900	2.0	7.1	6.3
Mortgage Bankers & Loan Corr	6162	2.4	3.9	9.0
Motion Pic, Videotape Prodtn	7812	12.4	18.4	11.1
Motion Pict, Videotape Distr	7822	5.7	9.0	30.0
Motor Vehicle Part, Accessory	3714	0.8	3.4	0.8
Motor Vehicles & Car Bodies	3711	2.3	22.2	7.7
Motorcycles, Bicycles & Parts	3751	1.4	5.6	11.8
Newspaper: Pubg, Pubg & Print	2711	4.0	10.7	6.7
Office Machines, Nec	3579	1.5	4.7	3.5
Offices of Medical Doctors	8011	1.2	6.1	16.4
Operative Builders	1531	1.0	8.9	−11.6
Operators—Nonres Bldgs	6512	3.6	9.2	5.1
Ophthalmic Goods	3851	9.1	15.5	9.8
Ortho, Prosth, Surg Appl, Suply	3842	2.9	6.0	23.7
Paints, Varnishes, Lacquers	2851	2.8	7.3	7.4
Paper & Paper Products—Whsl	5110	1.6	6.7	19.1
Paper Mills	2621	1.1	4.5	−2.0
Patent Owners and Lessors	6794	2.9	12.2	13.5
Pens, Pencils, Oth Office Matl	3950	5.7	12.5	8.2
Perfume, Cosmetic, Toilet Prep	2844	10.3	16.5	2.2

Industry	SIC No.	Ad $ as % Sales	Ad $ as % Margin	Annual Ad Growth Rate %
Periodical: Pubg & Print	2721	7.6	16.4	16.4
Personal Credit Institutions	6141	1.1	2.9	–7.7
Personal Services	7200	4.5	12.7	5.5
Petroleum Refining	2911	1.0	6.7	17.5
Pharmaceutical Preparations	2834	5.9	8.1	6.8
Phone Comm Ex Radiotelephone	4813	2.1	4.4	6.0
Phono Recrds, Audio Tape, Disk	3652	13.8	29.2	15.9
Photofinishing Laboratories	7384	4.0	11.4	8.2
Photographic Equip & Suppl	3861	4.3	10.4	6.4
Plastic Matl, Synthetic Resin	2820	1.3	4.3	10.8
Plastics Products, Nec	3089	2.3	6.0	5.3
Plastics, Resins, Elastomers	2821	0.7	2.2	–0.9
Poultry Slaughter & Process	2015	2.3	16.3	11.4
Prepackaged Software	7372	3.9	5.5	16.9
Printing Trades Machy, Equip	3555	2.2	5.3	4.8
Prof & Coml Eq & Supply—Whsl	5040	2.1	6.4	5.1
Public Bldg & Rel Furniture	2531	0.7	5.5	7.6
Pumps and Pumping Equipment	3561	1.4	4.4	–2.1
Radio, TV Broadcast, Comm Eq	3663	1.2	3.3	6.0
Radio, TV Cons Electr Stores	5731	4.1	18.3	8.3
Radiotelephone Communication	4812	2.9	5.6	13.7
Real Estate Investment Trust	6798	0.6	1.0	0.5
Refrig & Service Ind Machine	3580	1.9	6.0	1.3
Retail Stores	5990	3.7	8.1	12.9
Rubber and Plastics Footwear	3021	5.5	13.6	12.8
Sausage, oth Prepared Meat Pd	2013	9.0	23.3	8.7
Savings Instn, Fed Chartered	6035	0.9	2.2	–8.0
Security Brokers & Dealers	6211	2.2	8.4	–3.6
Semiconductor, Related Device	3674	1.9	4.1	15.1
Sheet Metal Work	3444	2.9	9.9	–13.3
Ship & Boat Bldg & Repairing	3730	4.2	34.3	–6.6
Skilled Nursing Care Fac	8051	2.1	17.5	5.1
Soap, Detergent, Toilet Preps	2840	9.1	21.0	10.4
Spec Outpatient Facility, Nec	8093	1.0	4.8	11.5
Special Clean, Polish Preps	2842	16.8	28.8	6.9
Special Industry Machinery	3550	5.5	17.0	–0.6
Special Industry Machy, Nec	3559	1.0	2.4	0.1

Industry	SIC No.	Ad $ as % Sales	Ad $ as % Margin	Annual Ad Growth Rate %
Sporting & Athletic Gds, Nec	3949	4.1	10.3	13.2
Srch, Det, Nav, Guid, Aero Sys	3812	0.3	1.0	0.4
Sugar & Confectionery Prods	2060	10.9	26.6	7.1
Surgical, Med Instr, Apparatus	3841	1.3	2.6	11.7
Svc to Motion Picture Prodtn	7819	3.4	10.7	5.9
Svcs to Dwellings, Oth Bldgs	7340	1.6	5.5	3.9
Tele & Telegraph Apparatus	3661	0.6	1.6	−19.5
Television Broadcast Station	4833	3.1	8.4	4.4
Textile Mill Products	2200	1.0	4.2	0.6
Tires and Inner Tubes	3011	2.5	8.5	3.7
Unsupp Plastics Film & Sheet	3081	3.5	10.4	−2.3
Variety Stores	5331	1.6	6.9	6.2
Video Tape Rental	7841	2.9	6.1	18.0
Water Transportation	4400	7.6	19.8	2.3
Wmns, Miss, Chld, Infnt Undgrmt	2340	3.8	9.3	7.4
Women's Clothing Stores	5621	3.1	8.2	6.8
Womens, Misses, Jrs Outerwear	2330	2.9	9.0	10.5
Wood Hshld Furn, Ex Upholsrd	2511	4.0	11.3	8.7

Note: *Advertising Ratios & Budgets* covers over 400 industries. The 200 industries listed here were selected as the industries with the largest dollar volume of advertising based on estimated 1993 spending. For information about other industries, contact Schonfeld & Associates, Inc.

Legend: SIC No. = Standard Industrial Classification Number
Ad $ as % Sales = Advertising / Net Sales
Ad $ as % Margin = Advertising Expense / (Net Sales—Cost of Goods Sold)
Annual Ad Growth rate % = Average Annual Compound Growth Rate in Ad Spending

Source: *Advertising Ratios & Budgets,* Seventeenth Edition, published by Schonfeld & Associates, Inc., 1 Sherwood Drive, Lincolnshire, Illinois 60069, (708) 948-8080. 207 pages. Price $325.

MARKETING BOOT CAMP

Success   #**15**   Strategy

The Lucrative Benefit Of Benefits

Understanding the difference between features and benefits is crucial to your success. Please pay close attention. **Features** are about you and your product or service (what it is). **Benefits** are the specific *results* your product or service offers to your client or prospect (what it does). Just look at the marketing materials you receive. Most of them are selfish monologues instead of problem-solving dialogues. Or worse, they're just plain boring. Why do these documents inevitably fail? Because they don't **immediately** address the buyer's critical self-interest questions: "So What?", "Who Cares?" or "What's In It For Me?" You see, people don't buy things, they buy *results* like happiness, making and saving money, saving time, popularity, wisdom, comfort, praise and recognition, attractiveness, safety, security and easier ways to do things. Technology may be changing our lifestyles, but our needs and wants have remained basically the same for millions of years. Thus, be sure all of your marketing materials include "payoff benefits" that *specifically* communicate how you can help people to:

Make money	Be comfortable	Make life easier
Save money	Love and be loved	Be safe and secure
Save time	Avoid effort	Keep possessions
Lessen work	Discover inner	Be entertained
Gain control	harmony	Become smarter
Be popular	Be admired	Gain power, status
Be more attractive	Gain praise and	Exploit opportunities
Be healthier	recognition	Avoid criticism
Stay younger	Avoid problems	Be more productive
Gain wisdom		

Never assume people can translate your features into benefits— you must always do this for them.

Case in point: An elderly man walked into a computer store and was approached by a salesmen who immediately launched into a monologue about the technological wizardry of a particular personal computer. The salesman was on a roll while his cornered prey listened patiently. About 20 minutes into the presentation, the man timidly asked if he could easily write letters to his grandchildren on the machine. That's all he *really* wanted to know! And that's the difference between features and benefits. The salesman failed to ask the right questions and went on and on about the features of the machine (what the computer could do) instead of uncovering and addressing the real benefits the man was seeking (what the computer could do for Grandpa). Do you see the difference? Remember: customer-oriented marketing *always* leads with benefits and follows with features. Also, never assume people can translate your features into benefits—you must always do this for them.

MARKETING BOOT CAMP

Success   #**16**   Strategy

Sell To Wants, Not Needs

We've all heard or read that the essence of marketing is to "find a need and fill it." Well, unless you have deep pockets or know exactly what the world needs, here's a fail-safe formula that will skyrocket your success:

Find a WANT and fill it.

You see, most of us have enough food, shelter, clothing and transportation. We don't *need* much more. But we *want* more. We need food but we *want* fast foods, diet foods and gourmet meals. We probably don't need a six-bedroom, 4 1/2 bath home but we may *want* one. We don't need expensive designer clothes but we *want* them. We probably need a car but we *want* a Lexus or a Lincoln. We don't need 60-minute audio tapes— we *want* to gain wisdom quickly and conveniently. We don't need insurance. We *want* security and protection. You get the picture.

Tipping The "Want" Scales
In Your Favor

Remember that people buy with their hearts (emotion) and then rationalize their decision with their heads (logic). So please, sell to people's wants (desires), not their needs (something required) and they'll reward you handsomely! How do you do this? By sincerely communicating "payoff benefits" (see Success Strategy #15) and how your product or service can satisfy the three most important human emotions of hope, admiration and fear.

MARKETING BOOT CAMP

Success   #**17**   Strategy

Create The Payoff Picture In Their *Minds*

People don't buy for rational reasons, they buy for emotional rewards. Your marketing returns will take a quantum leap forward if you can help your prospects **project or see themselves already using or enjoying your product or service.** In other words, tap into their subconscious yearnings to create or feed a desire.

Pushing Emotional Buttons

In many cases your marketing message will have little to do with your specific product or service. Your goal is to help people to *imagine* how your product or service will enhance their quality of life.

For example, if you're marketing enhanced presentation skills workshops to professionals, make them see, hear and feel the *experience* of receiving a standing ovation! If you're selling a boat, use a photograph or video to show it cutting through the waves with elated people on board. A portrait photographer doesn't just create beautiful pictures—he or she preserves moments and everlasting *feelings* to love and treasure. If you save people money, don't just tell them how much. Show them exactly what the extra savings will buy them. Perhaps it's their dream vacation home, a college education for their children or a comfortable early retirement. People want to be rich, beautiful, happy, powerful, admired and smart. They also want to avoid losing what they already have. Now, look at the list of "payoff benefits" (Success Strategy #15) and help your consumer and business-to-business buyers see themselves already using and enjoying the rewards that your product or service brings to their lives.

MARKETING BOOT CAMP

Success   #**18**   Strategy

Positioning . . .
The Difference Between Profitability And Just "Getting By"

Do you know what the Marines want? A few good men and women, right? How about the Air Force? You're probably not sure. That's because the Marines have relentlessly utilized a simple yet potent marketing tool. And the Air Force hasn't. It's called *positioning,* and you too can use this powerful concept to create consistent top-of-mind awareness with your prospective customers.

Positioning's not something you do to your product or service, but something you do to the *mind* of your prospect. How about 7-Up? It can't beat Pepsi or Coke in the cola wars, so it's positioned as "the Uncola." How about Nyquil? It's the *night time* cold medicine. The "We're Number Two, But We Try Harder" position is a classic marketing victory in the battle for the mind and market share. And we'll bet you remember who said it. You see, in our media-numbed society, your message has to find a place in your prospect's already crammed cranium. So, the simpler your message, the better. What we're really talking about here is your *Unique Selling Position* (USP). That is, what unique **advantage(s)** can you offer that your competitors are not. The good news for you is that most businesses have not articulated a memorable USP.

Now is your opportunity to define or redefine *your* unique selling position to distinguish your enterprise from the pack and give consumers a *reason* to patronize you. Once you decide, you must integrate your USP into all of your marketing materials. It's an exercise that requires cerebral sweat equity, but the payoff is being remembered at the crucial time when your prospect is ready to buy.

Caution: Be sure to communicate *specific* positioning examples. For instance, telling someone you're more convenient than others is not as persuasive as saying you offer evening and week-end hours, plus 24-hour ordering and emergency service.

Now, what are the greatest values, benefits or specific advantages you can communicate to your customers and clients that will *differentiate* your product or service most successfully from your competitors?

- ➪ Do you save people time or money?
- ➪ Do you make people money?
- ➪ Do you offer a larger selection?
- ➪ Are you more convenient?
- ➪ Do you offer free installation?
- ➪ Are you more expensive, less expansive?
- ➪ Do you offer better, faster service—same-day shipping, etc.?
- ➪ Do you guarantee the lowest price?
- ➪ Do you offer a stronger guarantee?
- ➪ Do you possess technology that allows you to respond faster to your customer's needs and wants?
- ➪ Are you more convenient: weekend, evening hours, 24-hour ordering?
- ➪ Do you give more than everyone else? Two-for-one or three-for-two specials?

Here are several successful USP examples you're probably familiar with to jump-start your thinking:

Clairol makes you look younger.
Paine Webber makes you richer.
Mercedes means safety and status.
Volvo is durable.
Budget Motel is economical.
Domino's pizza is fast.
Allstate inspires trust.
7-11 offers convenience.
Hallmark sends love.

Let's say you're a psychologist. You could position yourself as the expert in *female* mental health. Even though most psychology patients *are* women you're the one who **says it!**

To effectively expand your market, you can create an additional positioning name to your company. All you have to do is create a new *division* that speaks directly to your target audience. Let's say you're a financial planner doing business as Sally R. Smith & Associates and you've set your sights on getting more dental clients. Simply create and name a division called *Dental Practitioners Financial Services* and print up new letterhead. That way, you'll be instantly recognized as a company that understands and serves the unique financial challenges and opportunities faced by dental professionals. Do you see how positioning is not as much about your product or service as it is about **specific** benefits delivered?

Save People Time
And You'll Make More Money

With so many working couples, discretionary time is almost nonexistent. Anything you can do to save people time will be rewarded. QVC Network, Inc., a home shopping television program, invites you to buy products from the convenience of your home. Of course fast-food establishments are big business, but now "Take-Out Taxi" will pick up and deliver your carry-out order from restaurants that do not offer delivery. A telephone company lets you pay your bills by phone using a light pen, while a major food chain lets you order your groceries via an 800 number and delivers them to you. Meanwhile, shuttle-bus transportation companies are springing up all over the country to transport Johnny and Mary to trumpet lessons and soccer practice.

What's YOUR Promotable Edge?

What do your products or services do better, faster or cheaper than anyone else's? Now get busy and start writing down and communicating *your* unique advantages.

MARKETING BOOT CAMP

Success   #**19**   Strategy

Irresistible Offers:
The Siren's Song To Faster Sales

"Master marketers motivate people to take action in their best interest . . . NOW!"

That sage advice offered by Dr. Jeffrey Lant, one of today's top authors, educators and marketing practitioners, sums up the essence of effective marketing. Your mission is to get your prospects or clients to **act on your offer** *sooner* **than later.** That means using *interactive* marketing techniques that ask them to write, phone, request free literature, take advantage of a free initial consultation or seminar program, return a coupon or send a check. Remember, your prospects need (and like) to be given clear, precise directions and it's **your** job to tell them what to do!

People don't like to change or try new products and ideas. If you're convinced that your product or service can help them (and you'd better have that conviction or your sales will suffer), it's to your advantage *and* the benefit of your prospects to motivate them to try your offering *now!* Unfortunately, people are slow to move. Most will not respond to your first offerings. But that's exactly why your *"9/18" Relationship Marketing System* is up and running, right? It's up to you to tell your prospects, clients and customers what you want them to do and to make it *easy* for them to do it.

Rewards Give Them A Reason To Read, Listen And Act FASTER!

A publisher offered university professors a choice between an attractive pen and an abacus if they would read several chapters of an innovative computer textbook, provide their comments in writing, and return a survey card by a particular date. The promotion worked like a dream. It prodded the professors to open the book, read the chapters and consider a new way of presenting introductory computer curricula. Additionally, thousands of cards were returned and the publisher's salespeople, armed with each professor's favorable comments or concerns, were able to gauge their prospects' degree of interest and answer objections faster.

Your Offers Must Be Relevant

Try to create offers and premiums that will logically tie in to your product or service. Can you see how the pen and abacus mentioned above were appropriate premiums for professors in the textbook market? Offers and premiums are only limited by your imagination. Here are several examples to stimulate your thinking and rocket your response rate:

- Offer free consultations, examinations, seminars, estimates, demonstrations, catalogs, samples, gifts and survey reports.
- Ask for action—write, phone, request free literature.
- Provide a money-back guarantee.
- Announce limited qualities.
- Use "bill me later" statements (however, give them something extra if they pay with cash now. *Success* magazine is giving away a free motivational book when you pay with cash to renew your subscription).
- Use early-bird discounts.
- Offer "mystery" gifts.
- Offer private sales or charter memberships.
- Promote limited time offers.

↪ Offer free special report, booklet, book, audio/videotape, or checklist (e.g., *17 Ways To Boost Direct Mail Response; Money-Saving Negotiating Tips For Meeting Planners*).

↪ Make one-time only offers.

↪ Use referral gifts.

↪ Offer multiple gift premiums.

↪ Use sweepstakes and contests.

↪ Include a detached reply device.

↪ Use involvement devices like check-off boxes.

↪ Provide free shipping.

↪ Offer a bulk-purchase discount.

↪ Make a get acquainted offer—3 free widgets—can cancel after that.

↪ Use 800 number answerlines or hotlines.

Why are offers so effective? Think about human nature. People naturally respond better to deadline pressure (remember exams?) and will act faster if they feel they're going to lose out on something. So, whenever possible, try to create a sense of urgency with time-limited, product-limited, one-time-only offers and fast-response discounts to boost your chances for greater responses and results.

MARKETING BOOT CAMP

Success #**20** Strategy

The 13 Crucial Questions You Must Answer Before Writing Any Marketing Document

It's counterproductive (and costly) to begin writing your ads, flyers, sales letters, brochures, catalogs, etc., until you know your exact target audience and the precise advantages your product or service can offer them. What's more, if you're ever on a tight deadline, this Q & A process can prevent anxiety and help you work smarter and faster under tight deadlines. Therefore, it's crucial that you answer these questions—in writing—before you begin.

1. Whom are you trying to reach?
2. What is the competitive situation?
3. What specific benefits are you offering them?
4. What proof do you have to substantiate your benefits?
5. Why should your prospects buy now?
6. What will happen if they don't?
7. What obstacles are preventing them from buying?
8. What do you want the prospect to do?
9. How do you want them to do it?
10. What media are involved?
11. What is your budget?
12. What are your sales objectives?
13. Are testimonials or case histories available?

MARKETING BOOT CAMP

Success **#21** Strategy

Simplify Your Writing For Maximum Impact

Many times our marketing messages don't come across with the impact we want because of the way they are written. One of the major reasons is wordiness. Try to eliminate wordiness in everything you write. Quarrel with the need for every paragraph, every sentence, every word. The longer you take to say things, the more you blur your ideas. When deadlines permit, let your writing rest for a day and then rewrite it. And rewrite it. To help you clean up your wordiness and make your writing livelier and your ideas clearer, use the following words:

Instead of	Try
accompany	go with
accomplish	carry out, do
accomplish (a form)	fill out
accordingly	so
accrue	add, gain
accurate	correct, exact, right
achieve	do, make
actual	real
additional	added, more, other
address	discuss
addressees are requested	(omit), please
adjacent to	next to
advantageous	helpful
advise	recommend, tell
afford an opportunity	allow, let
aircraft	plan
anticipate	expect
a number of	some
apparent	clear, plain
appear	seem
appreciable	many
appropriate	(omit), proper, right
approximately	about
as a means of	to
ascertain	find out, learn
as prescribed by	under
assist, assistance	aid, help

Instead of	Try
attached herewith is	here's
attempt	try
at the present time	now
be advised	(omit)
be responsible for	handle
benefit	help
by means of	by, with
capability	ability, can
category	class, group
caveat	warning
close proximity	near
cognizant	aware, responsible
combined	joint
comply with	follow
component	part
comprise	form, include, make up
concerning	about, on
conclude	close, end
concur	agree
confront	face, meet
consequently	so
consolidate	combine, join, merge
constitutes	is, forms, makes up
construct	build
contains	has

Instead of	Try
continue	keep on
contribute	give
current	(omit)
deem	think
delete	cut, drop
demonstrate	prove, show
depart	leave
designate	appoint, choose, name
desire	wish
determine	decide, figure, find
develop	grow, make, take place
disclose	show
discontinue	drop, stop
disseminate	issue, send out
do not	don't
due to the fact that	due to, since
echelons	levels
effect	make
elect	choose, pick
eliminate	cut, drop, end
employ	use
encounter	meet
encourage	urge
endeavor	try
ensure	make sure
enumerate	count
environment	(omit)
equitable	fair
equivalent	equal
establish	set up, prove, show
evaluate	check, rate, test
evidenced	showed
evident	clear
examine	check, look at
exhibit	show
expedite	hurry, rush, speed up
expeditious	fast, quick
expend	pay out, spend
expense	cost, fee, price
expertise	ability, skill
explain	show, tell
facilitate	ease, help
factor	reason, cause
failed to	didn't
feasible	can be done, workable
females	women
final	last
finalize	complete, finish
for a period of	for
for example	such as
forfeit	give up, lose
for the purpose of	for, to
forward	send

Instead of	Try
function	act, role, work
furnish	give, send
herein	here
however	but
identical	same
identify	find, name, show
immediately	at once
impacted	affected, changed, hit
implement	carry out, do, follow
in accordance with	by, following, under
in addition	also, besides, too
in an effort to	to
inasmuch as	since
in a timely manner	on time, promptly
inception	start
in conjunction with	with
in consonance with	agree with
incorporate	blend, join, merge
incumbent upon	must
indicate	show, write down
indication	sign
initial	first
initiate	start
in lieu of	instead of
in order that	for, so
in order to	to
in regard to	about, concerning, on
inter alia	(omit)
interface with	deal with, meet
interpose no objection	don't object
in the amount of	for
in the course of	during, in
in the event that	if
in the near future	soon
in view of	since
in view of the above	so
it is	(omit)
it is essential	must
it is recommended	we recommend
it is requested	please, we request
justify	prove
legislation	law
liaise with	coordinate, talk with
limited number	few
limitations	limits
locate	find
location	place, scene, site
magnitude	size
maintain	keep, support
majority	greatest, longest, most
methodology	method
minimize	decrease, lessen, reduce

Instead of	Try
modify	change
monitor	check, watch
month of	(omit)
nebulous	vague
necessitate	cause, need
non-concur	disagree
notify	let know, tell
not later than	by
numerous	many, most
objective	aim, goal
obligate	bind, compel
observe	see
obtain	get
on a ___ basis	(omit)
operate	run, work
operational	working
optimum	best, greatest, most
option	choice, way
parameters	limits
participate	take part
perform	do
permit	let
personnel	people, staff
pertaining to	about, of, on
point in time	point, time
portion	part
position	place, put
possess	have, own
practicable	practical
preclude	prevent
prepared	ready
previous	earlier, past
previously	before
prioritize	rank
prior to	before
probability	chance
procedures	rules, ways
proceed	do, go on, try
proficiency	skill
programmed	planned
promulgate	announce, issue
provide	give, say, supply
provided that	if
provides guidance for	guides
provisions of	(omit)
purchase	buy
purpose is to	(omit)
pursuant to	by, following, under
reason for	why
recapitulate	sum up
reduce	cut
reflect	say, show
regarding	about, of, on
relating to	about, on
relocation	move
remain	stay

Instead of	Try
remainder	rest
remuneration	pay, payment
render	give, make
request	ask
require	must, need
requirement	need
reside	live
retain	keep
review	check, go over
selection	choice
shall	will
shortfall	shortage
similar to	like
solicit	ask for
state	say
state-of-the-art	latest
subject	the, this, your
submit	give, send
subsequent	later, next
subsequently	after, later, then
substantial	large, real, strong
sufficient	enough
take action to	(omit), please
task	ask
terminate	end, stop
that	(omit)
therefore	so
there are	(omit), exist
therein	there
there is	(omit), exists
thereof	its, their
this command	us, we
timely	prompt
time period	(either one)
transmit	send
transpire	happen, occur
-type	(omit)
until such time as	until
(the) use of	(omit)
utilize, utilization	use
validate	confirm
value	cost, worth
verbatim	word for word, exact
viable	practical, workable
vice	instead of, versus
warrant	call for, permit
whenever	when
whereas	since
with reference to	about
with the exception of	except for
witnessed	saw
your office	you
/	and, or

MARKETING BOOT CAMP

Success #**22** Strategy

Write This Way To More Sales

When creating direct response marketing documents—ads, sales letters, self-mailing brochures and the like, use this time-proven formula to generate results. It's called AIDA (pronounced Ā-Da), an acronym for Attention, Interest, Desire and Action—and it works!

- ⇨ **Attention.** Hit readers with an **attention-getting headline** to pull them into your document. Use your most important benefit or promise, offer, quote, question, challenge, news, value or statistics. You've only got 2–5 seconds to grab them by the lapels and pull them into your message. Most readers never get past the headline so you've got to answer those self-critical questions fast: "So What?", "Who Cares?", "What's In It For Me?"
- ⇨ **Interest.** Hit a nerve: pose a problem your prospect is experiencing and then agitate the problem; be specific about what the reader will get or how your product or service will help them. Provide proof with endorsements, guarantees or testimonials. Avoid generalities. Sell people the benefits or advantages your product or service offers.
- ⇨ **Desire.** Get people emotionally involved, make them say "yes this is me," let them see themselves already using, enjoying and benefiting from your product or service. Touch on their deepest aspirations or anxieties. Get them beyond "I Like It" to "I Want It!"
- ⇨ **Action.** Ask for the order! Provide a specific reward or urgent reason to incite immediate action like limited-time offers or limited availability.

Copywriting Tips

When you write marketing materials, you're not talking to a group of people. It's one-on-one communication. Check out the following strategies.

➪ Make your writing sound **personal,** just like you're telling someone about your product or service face-to-face.

➪ Be sure you write in the language your audience understands.

➪ Use active words in the present tense.

➪ Be upbeat! Positive copy almost always outpulls negative copy.

➪ Use the word YOU and plenty of benefits. Examples: "you get," "you save," "you will receive," "you will accomplish," etc.

➪ Readers are lazy; make it easy for them to understand and respond. Write in a clear style an 8th grader could read.

➪ In direct mail, try to involve your reader with tokens, check-off boxes, true-or-false quizzes, scratch-and-sniff devices and the like to get them actively involved.

➪ Indent paragraphs.

➪ Use short sentences. Like this.

➪ Include visual eye-catchers like boxes □, bullets •, arrows ➪, ALL CAPS, *italics,* <u>underlines</u>, and **boldface** or a second color for your subheadlines.

The Powerful P.S.

Always use a postscript in a sales letter because it's *always read*. Studies show that most readers will skim through a sales letter in this fashion before they devote time to read the entire document: They'll glance at the headline, the salutation, the signature (to see who it's from) and then go the P.S. An effective P.S. can repeat your primary benefit or offer, introduce a surprise bonus or restate your iron-clad guarantee, or pull them back into the body copy of the letter with a statement like, "as I said in paragraph four about the specific money-making potential of this breakthrough software."

How Long Should Your Copy Be?

As long as it takes to get your reader to act. The typical objection to long copy is that "no one reads it." Listen. We've written 4-, 8-, even 16-page sales letters that have been highly profitable. People *will* read long copy if they're interested in the subject. Consider this: If you were selling your product or service face-to-face with a prospect, would you stop after the first page of your presentation? Think back to the last time you bought a new car or computer, or whatever. If you're like us, you probably pored over every ad and read every brochure or specification sheet from cover to cover because you were hungry to learn more about it, and to logically justify your potential emotionally driven purchase. As a general guideline, short copy tends to be more effective for lead generation while longer copy ("the more you tell the more you sell") is typically used for generating orders.

Make Your Advertising Pay!

For any letter, flyer, or brochure there are five steps to make your advertising work harder for you.

1. **Get Attention.** Four out of five people will not read below the headline . . . unless you can create interest. Headlines such as "Speak and Grow Rich," "Turn Your Hobby Into Dollars," and "Are You a Failure at 30?" get the attention of the reader, so he or she will read on.

2. **Show Benefits—WIIFM, or What's In It For Me?** Stress the benefits people get versus the features. For example, people don't buy a drill (feature), but the hole (benefit) that it makes. An accountant doesn't sell tax preparation (feature) but peace of mind (benefit). Focus on what people can save, gain or accomplish by using your product or service.

3. **Establish Credibility.** People ultimately deal with you for two reasons . . . because they trust you and like you. Develop trust and likability in your marketing materials by adding testimonials, information on your expertise, quotes from you featured in magazines or newspapers, a list of customers, the number of customers you have, pictures of you at work and number of years in business.

4. **Make an Offer.** People need incentives to act. Use "limited time offers." "special prices" and "book me now because my speaking schedule fills up fast" strategies.

5. **Call for Action.** Make it easy for the customer to respond to you. Your phone number and address should be easily seen and understood. An optometrist client of ours lost many potential patients because they couldn't find his office. Only when he mentioned in his advertising that his office was next to the McDonalds did it become clear where he was located.

This sales referral letter (below) and response coupon (on the following page) were accompanied by a case study (see #31). Thus far the builder is enjoying a 6:1 Return on Investment (ROI) from this direct response package, with sales and referrals still coming in.

Design ▢ Remodeling

Here are 3 Valuable Reasons...

why YOU should spend a few minutes on the phone with me, or mail the enclosed card BEFORE you hire a Design/Remodeling firm for your next home remodeling project.

And when you retain our services, we'll thank you with a charming cedar Adirondack Rocking Chair (or, if you're not considering a project right now, we'll give you this valuable free gift when you refer us to someone who does.)

Dear Homeowner,

If you've been contemplating a design and remodeling project to make your home bigger, brighter and more beautiful, it will benefit you to read this letter very carefully.

Imagine enjoying "new home" features like huge Palladian windows to brighten your living room or foyer—or adding a family room with a cathedral ceiling and warm cozy fireplace. And just think about the ooooh's and aaaah's you'll hear when family and friends see your stunning new spacious kitchen!

Well, now you *can* enjoy a fresh new look that perfectly matches your taste and your budget. I'd like to tell you about the *advantages* **Gilday Design/Remodeling** can bring to your next remodeling project.

1. We *guarantee* your satisfaction.
Our 16-year reputation for reliability and two-year warranty on all work and installations stand behind each and every job. Further, *you have my promise* that we will find the most creative and efficient ways to design and complete your project and to assure lasting *value* for your most important investment.

2. Here's why people keep coming to us... and why you should.
We invite you to visit one of our completed projects to *see* the expert craftsmanship and the careful attention that has been paid to every construction detail. Plus, our large and growing file of testimonial letters like this one from the Coburns of Washington, DC confirms the high customer satisfaction we achieve on *every* project.

> *"Thank you for the outstanding job you did in remodeling our kitchen and front entrance. The design is excellent and the work is the highest quality. We are enjoying the kitchen very much and have received many compliments on it. Moreover, you managed to stay within the time you alloted. We are extremely pleased with the project (the fourth you have done for us). We look forward to working with you again in the future."*

3. Remodeling Expertise – all under one roof – to make your life easier.
Our team of in-house residential specialists include award-winning architects, kitchen and bath designers and master carpenters. If at any time you have a problem or concern, one simple call to us will bring you a quick and courteous response.

Even if you're only *thinking* about a remodeling project, I invite you to call me or return the enclosed card. It's your chance to talk with a professional, evaluate your home's creative potential, discuss your special needs and preferences, and get a free, no-obligation estimate.

So take a moment now and call me at **301/565-4600** or mail back the enclosed card while you're thinking about it. I guarantee I'll open your eyes to the beautiful and exciting *new* possibilities we could add to your home!

Cordially,

Tom Gilday

Thomas A. Gilday
Vice President

P.S. You can expect an immediate "payback" on your remodeling project because home improvements are one of today's most *visible* ways to increase the value of your home.

Remember, the beautiful cedar Adirondack Rocking Chair is yours when you retain Gilday Remodeling services. And even if you're not considering a project now, when you refer someone who becomes a remodeling client with Gilday, we'll thank you both with these attractive chairs absolutely free! Just call me at **301/565-4600** or return the postage-free card **before May 31, 1993** to qualify.

Call Tom Gilday at 301/565-4600 or return this card before May 31, 1993 to qualify for your free cedar Adirondack Rocking Chair.

Free Remodeling Consultation and Gift Offer.
☐ YES, Tom, I want to save time, money and headaches on my next remodeling job. Please call me about the design/remodeling project we've been considering. I understand there's no obligation for your advice and free estimate and that I will receive a charming cedar Adirondack Rocking Chair when we work together on a $10,000+ project.

Special Referral Gift Offer.
☐ SORRY, Tom, we won't be doing any home repair or remodeling projects until (Date) _____. But I *really* would love to have one of those cedar Adirondack Rocking Chairs for my backyard or porch. Here are the names of people I know who might be in the market for your remodeling services. I understand that if they sign on with you for a $10,000+ project, the chair is mine!

Free Money-Saving Special Reports.
☐ YES, Tom, please place me on your interested customer list to receive by mail your complimentary Special Reports. I want to learn how to increase the value of my home through state-of-the-art design and remodeling techniques.

Name _____

Address _____

City _____ State _____ Zip _____

Day Phone _____ Evening Phone _____

Referral Name _____ Day Phone / Evening Phone _____

Referral Name _____ Day Phone / Evening Phone _____

NO POSTAGE
NECESSARY
IF MAILED
IN THE
UNITED STATES

BUSINESS REPLY MAIL
FIRST CLASS PERMIT NO. 6090 SILVER SPRING, MD

POSTAGE WILL BE PAID BY ADDRESSEE

Gilday Design/Remodeling
9162 Brookville Road
Silver Spring, MD 20910-9784

Reprinted with permission from Gilday Design & Remodeling. Graphic design by Mary Byrd Productions. Copy by Dan McComas Associates.

MARKETING BOOT CAMP

Success #**23** Strategy

"Hot-Button" Headlines That Get Attention

Good headlines can boost your response by 100% to 500%.

However, 80% of readers never get past a marketing document's headline if it's poorly written. But this won't happen to you when you make a promise, offer a benefit or present news that will give your audience what they want. Statement headlines are typically stronger than question headlines. Why? Because you don't want your reader to answer the headline with a "no," a "maybe" or an "I don't know." Question headlines can be effective, however, if you genuinely know the problems or wants of your target audience, or when posed as a curiosity headline like, "Why aren't all financial planners rich?"

Dan's introduction to Dr. Jeffrey Lant was through a postcard deck card with a headline that read: *"Hey Marketing And Sales Execs, If You're So Smart, How Come You're Not Making A Six-Figure + Salary Right Now!"* This "challenge" headline motivated Dan to immediately call Jeffrey and order two of his marketing books (and several more after that!). Also, steer clear of clichés, cute or "clever" headline copy. It will only distract or confuse your reader. Your job is to get people to agree with you and to act! The *italicized* words below are proven headline attention-getters. Use them to boost your response:

How To Win Friends And Influence People

Secrets Of Successful Consultants

Warning: Poor Customer Service Is Hazardous To Your Bottom Line!

Are You Getting The Most Computer Power For Your Dollar?

10 *Ways, (Tips or Hints) To* Save Money On Your Taxes

Introducing The Newest Energy-Saving Device From Myer Electronics

Announcing The Latest Breakthrough In Catalog Shopping

Attention: Video Producers In Need Of More Sales

We Guarantee The New XYZ Fax Will Save You $75 A Month

What Could You Do With An Extra $25,000 to $100,000?

For Busy Salesmen *Only:* How To Make More Sales In Less Time

Now You Can Clean Windows Faster and Easier

7 *Advantages You Get* With Jenkins Auto Leasing

Who Needs Better Gas Mileage?

What You Should Know About Financial Planning

The Easy Way To A Healthier Lifestyle

Discover How Realtors Are Making More Sales With The "Breakthrough Farming" System

11 *Reasons Why* More Plumbers Are Now Turning To Smith Supply Company

Promising New Breakthrough In Mental Health Care

The Truth About Workaholics

"10 Marketing *Mistakes You Can Avoid* Right Now."

Hint: Author and lecturer Ted Nicholas notes that headlines containing quote marks like the one above draw 28% more attention. He says this happens because the words are perceived to be more important when someone appears to be quoted. Why not test your next direct response ad or sales letter headline with and without quote marks and see for yourself?

MARKETING BOOT CAMP

Success #**24** Strategy

Power Words That Pull

To get and keep your reader's or listener's attention and interest, work these motivating words into your marketing copy:

Acclaimed	Hurry	Remarkable
Advancement	Imagine	Results
Amazing	Important	Revolutionary
Announcing	Improved	Safety
Astonishing	Incredible	Sale
At Last	Instantly	Save
Attention	Introducing	Secret
Bargain	Last Chance	Sensational
Boosts	Love	Simplifies
Breakthrough	Miracle	Special Offer
Challenge	Money-Making	Startling
Choice	Money-Saving	Striking
Compare	New	Suddenly
Delivers	Now	Sure-Fire
Discount	Offer	Surprising
Discover	Plus	The Truth About
Easy	Power	Trusted
Effective	Practical	Ultimate
Exceptional	Prevents	Valuable
Extraordinary	Profitable	Wanted
Free	Proven	Warning
First Time Ever	Quickly	You
Guaranteed	Recommended	Yours
How To	Reliable	

MARKETING BOOT CAMP

Success   #**25**   Strategy

Extra! Extra! Editorial Ads Increase Readership

You see them all the time. Ads that don't look like ads but appear to be editorial copy or stories in the publication you're reading. Savvy marketers use this technique because they know people are five to nine times more likely to read "editorial" copy than a display ad. The "advertorial" (a hybrid of advertising and editorial) format works because readers *perceive* that your product or service is newsworthy. And with marketing, as with many things in life, perception is reality.

Advertorials are extremely effective as direct response vehicles. That is, you'll want to have a dashed border around a response coupon at the bottom of your ad or some kind of "marching orders" asking your prospects to write or phone. We've seen more and more businesses using this technique, but many are still not **asking their prospects to do something!** Look at *Success* and *Parade* magazines as well your trade publications for examples.

Hint: You may want to ask your advertising representative to place your advertorial ad inside an actual article. That way, the publication's editorial copy literally "wraps around" your ad and is virtually impossible to miss. The media won't always guarantee this placement, but you can request it.

This advertorial ad is putting sales on fast forward for this video producer.

Kids Have a Blast With New Road Construction Video
Award-Winning Tape A Surprise Smash Hit

MONTPELIER, Vt.—Independent video producer Fredric Levine is proving that you don't need high-tech special effects, animation or violence to hold kid's attention. Levine's award-winning release, *Road Construction Ahead*, is thrilling children, parents and grandparents across America with real-life images of the people and machines that build our roads.

Real Life Action Heroes

"I want to satisfy kids' curiosity about the working world around them," Levine says. His experience as a father of three young children has helped him to develop an eye for what kids like.

The result? A carefully produced, briskly edited, 30-minute tape that shows all the big machines kids love to watch. A friendly construction worker named George explains how the road

builders survey, excavate, blast, crush rocks, haul, grade, and pave a new highway.

"If your kids are fascinated by heavy equipment, then this video is for them."—United Media. Road Construction Ahead, $19.95 plus $3.95 shipping and handling from Focus Video, 1-800-843-3686.

Entertainment Industry Reaction

Since its release last year, *Road Construction Ahead* has sold over 100,000 copies. Levine's success has drawn the attention of the national media, including feature coverage by CBS's *Eye to Eye with Connie Chung* and ABC's *The Home Show.*

After viewing *Road Construction Ahead* with a group of preschoolers, Harry Smith, of *CBS*, said, "this is anything but the Saturday morning clatter kids are used to. Once your kids see this, they're mesmerized."

After Levine was interviewed on National Public Radio's *All Things Considered,* one station reported that the story generated more listener calls than any other broadcast in its history.

Parents and Grandparents Rave

Albert Vego of North Hills, Cal., wrote that his four-year-old grandson is "absolutely thrilled" with *Road Construction Ahead.* Janet Stavridge of Warminster, Pa., said that her two-year-old son "was totally engrossed from the first viewing."

Nancy Brian of Broken Arrow, Okla., wrote, *"Road Construction Ahead* has been played five times a day since it arrived....We appreciate the great camera work and editing, the attention to humans and machines, and the neat ending."

Producer Announces New Video

Using the same touch that earned Levine the California Children's

Media Award, the videomaker's newest release, *Fire & Rescue,* goes behind the scenes to give kids the thrill and excitement of a day on the job with real firefighters. The narrator, a friendly fireman named Mike, shows kids life at the fire station, on the job, and includes some important safety rules.

How To Order

Both *Road Construction Ahead* and *Fire & Rescue* are recommended for children ages 2 to 8. To order either video, call toll-free 1-800-843-3686 or send $19.95 per tape plus $3.95 shipping and handling to: Focus Video, Dept. W7A, 138 Main Street, Montpelier, VT 05602. Allow 14 days for delivery. 30-day money-back guarantee.

Courtesy of Focus on Kids, Montpelier, VT.

MARKETING BOOT CAMP

Success #**26** Strategy

Before You Invest . . . Test, Test, Test

The ultimate judge and jury of your marketing is the consumer. Always let the marketplace tell you what it wants—not what you think it wants. Marketing is not an exact science. That's why it's crucial to test your assumptions, your market and your marketing messages before you roll out a large mailing or invest a bundle on an advertising or direct mail campaign. It's much easier and faster to test if you're using direct response marketing because you're asking people to call you, stop by, send in a response card or connect with you via telephone.

Let's take a direct response ad as an example. One simple way to test its effectiveness is through an A/B split run. Many newspapers and magazines will allow you to run one ad in half of their issues and one in the other. For instance, you can code a display or mail order advertisement by adding Department "D" to your phone number or address to gauge response. You can also test which media are pulling best for you by coding your ads via publication and date. If you run in the *Washington Post,* for example, the code printed in the coupon text of your ad might read WP 8/31. For easier evaluation, test one copy, headline or offer element at a time. Advertising great John Caples in his book *"Tested Advertising Methods"* (Prentice Hall) reminds us to always test four factors:

1. **Copy**—what you say, your appeal, or promise, and how you express it
2. **Media**—the magazines, newspapers, broadcasting facilities and other vehicles that will carry your message

3. **Position**—where your ad appears in publications, what times during the day and what day of the week for broadcast messages
4. **Season**—which months are best

When testing direct mail, here are the four key elements in order of importance:

1. Your product or service
2. The list
3. Your offer
4. The copy

Of course there are many other variables you may need to test in your mailing pieces, like price, envelope size and color, teasers, letter length, lift letters, discount and credit terms, premiums, time-limits, number of elements in the package and so on.

If your mailing is small (less than 1,000)—if you're mailing to people who already know you, or you're in a rush to take advantage of a time-sensitive opportunity, you can usually forgo testing. However, you'll want to bring in a copywriter or direct response consultant to give you a "second opinion" on your marketing materials.

Once you know what works and what doesn't, you'll be able to hit the marketplace running with successful products, services, offers and messages that you can profit from over and over again.

Another eye-opening resource for testing and improving your mailings is René Gnam's *Direct Mail Workshop* by Prentice Hall.

Note: One of the costliest mistakes you can make is prematurely changing your ad or direct mail package because you get tired of it. Remember, you'll always get bored with your marketing before your target audience does. Why? You're focused on it and see it virtually every day, while your target audience only pays minimal attention.

Is Your Advertising Working?

As William Wrigley said, "I know that half of my advertising is wasted, but I don't know which half." To determine if *your* advertising is working, try the following strategies.

Put it aside—Read it the next day, "sleep on it," and crucial changes will become clear.

Have someone read your ad copy back to you—Watch their reactions as they read it. See if the key points are coming across and the "punch" is where it should be.

Get opinions—Show 2 different ad samples and get opinions from others on which one they like best and why.

Split-run test—This is where you run two ads, one a little different than the other, and then compare the results.

Competition tracking—Keep a file of competitor ads. If the same ad is running constantly, it is more than likely a winning ad.

Focus groups—This is where you bring in 8 to 12 participants to answer questions posed by a trained moderator. Focus groups are a popular form of qualitative research to help you identify and analyze your prospective customers' subjective decision-making process. They are typically held in a special room with a one-way mirror to observe the participants' reactions to your ads, ideas, new products and other marketing materials. Sessions usually last $1^1/_2$ to 2 hours and participants are usually paid for their time.

MARKETING BOOT CAMP

Success #*27* Strategy

Small Space Ads:
Landing More Leads For Less $$$

"Fractional" ads are smart, cost-effective tools for generating leads. You can arouse curiosity by offering people something to get them to phone, fax or write you. Here's an example to get you started.

Make $75,000 A Year As An Ad Copywriter!

Turn your love of writing into cash! Nationally-acclaimed author and ace advertising copywriter Dan McComas reveals all his inside secrets of success at his upcoming Washington, D.C. seminar. Call now for free, no-obligation details. Hurry! Seating is severely limited. **(301) 946-4284.**

Of course you'll need to follow-up these leads with a strong sales letter/response package.

Also consider low-cost classified space in newspapers, magazines and industry newsletters on a local, regional, national and international basis. Classified ads typically work best when targeted at business opportunity, automotive, real estate and employment prospects.

Classified Ad Examples

*FREE REPORT** reveals 10 ways to boost your direct mail response NOW! Call (301) 777-5859 24-hours a day.

*Earn $500 a week with your computer.** Call 1-800-333-2525 for FREE, no-obligation details!

If you're selling nationally through display and classified ads, you'll want to refer to the *Standard Rate And Data Services* book in your library for publications and the brokers who can save you money on larger media buys.

Here's an example of a small space advertorial format.

"300% Increase in Response"

That's what you'll get when you add an 800 number to your current marketing messages, according to author and marketing expert Gary Halbert. *The reason?* The '90s are fast-paced. People want it *right now*. So make it easy for them by providing a 24-hour toll-free number customers can call from their armchairs or desks.

But how can you *easily* handle the calls and orders? Use a proven service provided by *Perfect Response Company* (PRC) in Boulder, Colorado. PRC (14 years of fulfillment service with 3,000+ satisfied clients) will take your incoming call, transcribe your caller's mailing info to a database and mail your materials or package the same day. *Cost?* 47¢ each. PRC can also process Visa and MasterCard purchases if your business doesn't have a merchant account. Call 1-800-889-1201 x 16 for info.

Reprinted with permission from The Business Center, Boulder, CO.

MARKETING BOOT CAMP

Success #**28** Strategy

The Effective Brochure . . . A Checklist

The most important concept to understand about the brochure is that it is your ambassador. Your brochure is what your prospective client has in front of him or her when you are not there to sell yourself or your product. It must be *first class* as it represents you and your company's skill, ability, quality and fitness for a proposed job or product sale.

To make sure your brochure is on target you must spend some time developing it. Even if you have a professional working on it follow these guidelines:

- ➪ Collect 30 or so brochures from different types of companies.
- ➪ Review them and analyze the various approaches that were taken. Study the copy, the pictures and the general layout.
- ➪ Separate the parts that you really like. Collect the best.
- ➪ Put the best parts in front of you and then do a rough pencil draft, combining the best elements.
- ➪ Build a few "dummy" brochures and then ask other people for opinions.

When developing and designing a brochure there are many key ingredients that should appear. Although not all of the elements below are necessary for each brochure, use this checklist to make sure you're on the right track. Some of the questions to ask yourself are:

Does the brochure match the visual and verbal image I want to project?

Does it state the who, what, where, when and how?

Does the front cover grab attention in a credible fashion to attract my audience, overcome their objections and entice them to open the brochure?

Does the headline get the attention of the reader?

Do I show credibility throughout the brochure?

Do I have testimonials?

Does it have pictures showing people "involved" with my product or service?

Does it stress the names or types of companies who have used my product or service?

Does it have quotes from the media?

Does it look too important for a secretary to throw away?

Do I sell the benefits throughout the brochure?

Do I use charts and graphs and other visuals where appropriate?

Do I provide a credible and even irresistible offer and guarantee?

Is it free of grammatical errors?

Is there plenty of white space?

Is it easy to read?

Does the message flow?

Do I treat the back cover as importantly as the front cover?

Do I use bold headlines and subheads to break up the copy and encourage prospects to read on?

Do my words sell? (i.e., active, specific, present-tense words promising results and benefits crucial to my target market?)

Do I make the brochure too valuable to throw away?

Do I provide and make prominent the special features of the services and products I offer?

Do I make it easy to get more information?

Are the address and phone number highlighted?

Does it ask the reader to take action?

MARKETING BOOT CAMP

Success **#29** Strategy

Testimonials . . . How To
Get Them . . . How To Use Them

As much as people like to think of themselves as individuals, most humans harbor a "herd mentality." When it comes to trying or buying something new, we like to know that others "tried it and liked it" first.

One of the most effective ways to lend credibility to your marketing and quiet all those "doubting Thomases" is through third-party endorsements or testimonials. Unsolicited, customer-written testimonials are typically the best because they come from the heart. But we'll bet that you have many satisfied clients who have never written a testimonial letter to you because:

a) you haven't asked them;
b) they don't have the time;
c) they don't know how to write one.

As you'll see, the most effective testimonials focus on the benefits that you or your product/service have brought to the lives of others. Here are some of the results-oriented points that can be communicated in a testimonial:

Service/Timeliness	Quality
Return On Investment Created	Accountability
Responsiveness	Durability
Reliability	Price
Special Abilities	Efficiency

Here's A Fast Way To Get A Powerful Testimonial

1. Call a satisfied client or customer (you do have one, don't you?). If you're a start-up business, ask someone whom you've benefited in a previous job or situation. Prospects are really buying YOU and your unique advantages. If you're selling a new product, use testimonials from your test or focus groups.

2. Tell them you're putting together your marketing materials and would like to include several comments from satisfied clients. Ask if this is OK. Almost everyone will say yes!

3. Don't ask questions that can be answered with a "yes" or "no." Ask your client open-ended questions like: Please tell me how our product/service specifically helped you achieve your goals? What did you like most about our product/service? How has our product/service benefited you or your buyers? Until they get warmed up, most people will give you general comments. That's when you say, "Could you be more *specific* about that?" An excellent last question to ask is, "Are there any other ways you can think of where our product/service has been beneficial?" Don't be surprised if you only have to ask one question and your client gives you everything you need. People like to feel important and talk about themselves!

4. Your clients will be presenting "stream of consciousness" comments so you'll need to take copious notes. After the conversation, tell them that you'll edit their comments for continuity and get back to them with a draft testimonial.

5. You'll probably have a page of comments to work from which you should boil down to about two to four sentences. Phone, fax or mail this draft back to your clients and ask them to initial it if OK or make any changes they like. In most cases they will immediately give you the green light and you'll have your testimonial.

6. Write out your testimonials in italic typeface (*like this*), or with quote marks (" ")—or both. Put your client's name, title, city and state under the testimonial. Try to get a minimum of three. The more the better. **Caution #1:** Be sure you have an OK in writing. **Caution #2:** Vary your testimonials to address the "results" points previously mentioned. The more ways you can prove your problem-solving capabilities, the more new business you will generate.

7. Now, include your proof-positive testimonials in all of your ads, sales letters, brochures and news releases.

Of course your testimonials don't have to come solely from your customers. You can also benefit from celebrity or public figure testimonials and endorsement letters; testimonials from technical experts or respected institutions and associations; editorial reviews, media quotes, reprints from newsletters and magazines; and the government. And don't worry about the effectiveness of testimonials over the years. Testimonials are timeless. It doesn't matter *when* you helped someone but *how* you helped them. Of course, you'll want to update your testimonials as you gain more satisfying results for your current customers or clients.

Incidently, calling customers for testimonials is a great way to re-connect with them and to generate repeat business.

Make Your Testimonials Specific and Results-Driven

Anemic:

"Your presentation was great!"

Stronger:

"In the three days since I attended your 'Call Reluctance' seminar, my appointments are up 30% and I've already closed two substantial deals. Thanks for helping me to identify and overcome my personal sales challenges and for your empathy and expertise!"

Anemic:

"Your news release really helped me generate a lot of media attention."

Stronger:

"Wow! In just two weeks your news release generated worldwide calls and letters, a three-minute TV interview, and a full-page COLOR newspaper spread. I literally received $5,000 of advertising for only $300!"

MARKETING BOOT CAMP

Success   #**30**   Strategy

Guarantees Ease The Buying Jitters

The marketplace is jaded. Skepticism is rampant. Thanks to unscrupulous politicians, marketers, even clergymen, to name a few, most of us have joined the ranks of the "burnt buyers" club. It's natural for your prospects to be wary of your offers and promises. Moreover, most people dread making decisions. They just don't like change, and when they do, they change very slowly. That's why believability is crucial. Therefore, it's incumbent upon you to show indisputable proof that your product or service will do what you say it will. One of the best ways to instill confidence is to include risk-reducers like:

- ⇨ Satisfaction guarantee
- ⇨ Unconditional money-back guarantee
- ⇨ Price protection guarantee
- ⇨ Life-time guarantee
- ⇨ Full-year warranty
- ⇨ No-quibble return policies
- ⇨ No-risk trial offers/send no money
- ⇨ Cancel at any time
- ⇨ Liberal return allowance
- ⇨ Your gift is tax-deductible

These strategies will help you overcome a prospect's reluctance to believe in you or buy from you. We guarantee it!

MARKETING BOOT CAMP

Success   #**31**   Strategy

Make A Case
Out Of Your Success Stories

People are fascinated by stories—especially tales of triumph.

Case studies are highly effective tools to demonstrate your problem-solving abilities. They're easy to write if you follow the three-step Problem-Action-Results (PAR) formula.

1. **Problem.** What was the problem your customer asked you to solve?
2. **Action.** What critical thinking, research or specific steps did you undertake to solve the problem or to help your customer reach a desired goal?
3. **Results.** What were the specific outcomes? How did your client benefit from the work that you did? What were his or her reactions to the good news?

You can include winning case studies or case histories in your ads, flyers, brochures and proposals.

Note: Some success story details may be confidential, so be sure to clear the copy with your client.

An example of a "before and after" case study for a builder. Notice the warm, "slice of life" tone and testimonial
to strengthen our client's story.

The Kamen's remodeling requests were typical of many Washington area homeowners. A small room and half bath were not being fully utilized due to their location and size limitations. Wanting to see the space put to a use for the whole family, the Kamens looked to Gilday Design/Remodeling for solutions.

Mr. Gilday and his staff architect visited the Kamen's home and listened to their requests. Using the budget constraints and their desired use of the new space, the sectioned off rooms were opened up to include a casual dining space with a desk and play area. The family could now dine, play and work together in an inviting light and open space.

To revitalize the kitchen area, four tall windows were installed plus white cabinets and light gray Corian countertops. The resulting room is flooded with natural sunlight and open views. Gilday completed the project by reinstalling the powder room conveniently off the main hall.

Gilday provides responsive design and remodeling solutions. Call Gilday today to schedule an appointment to review your remodeling wishes. Our first visit is always complementary.

"How perfect for our family. We want to thank you for a flawless design and execution."

Laurel Kamen
Vice President, Government Affairs
American Express Company
NW Washington, DC

■ Draw on our experience to build your dreams.

■ 9162 Brookville Road
Silver Spring, Maryland 20910
301 **565-4600**

Reprinted with permission from Gilday Design & Remodeling. Graphic design by Mary Byrd Productions. Copy by Dan McComas Associates.

MARKETING BOOT CAMP

Success   #**32**   Strategy

Newsletters: Subtle Sales Advice

Newsletters are subtle, yet seductive sales tools that help you stay connected with your target audiences. They reinforce the perception that you really know your business and that you care enough to communicate helpful advice on a regular basis.

Formats range from one-page sheets mailed every quarter to multi-page, multi-color monthly publications. For our purposes, we're talking about information-filled newsletters that you send to your prospects, clients and the media on a regular basis, free of charge. Fresh story angles and a clean, easy-to-read graphic design will increase readership. Plus, messages couched in an editorial format tend to achieve greater credibility and results.

Try incorporating several of these elements in your newsletter format to positively influence prospective customers and assist with customer retention.

1. New products
2. "How to" articles
3. Reprints of feature articles relevant to your target audience
4. Client profiles
5. Personnel profiles
6. Your success stories
7. New industry trends
8. Pending legislation
9. New clients being served
10. Survey questionnaires/survey results
11. Quizzes

You'll also want to encourage reader response by keeping your newsletter interactive. Offer special promotions, contests, drawings and advance-notice sales to increase letter, phone and fax responses. If your budget allows, you may want to personalize your newsletter with electronic printing similar to a concept being used on magazine covers. Several marketers are reporting increased response by including their customer's or prospect's name inside articles and even cartoon balloons.

MARKETING BOOT CAMP

Success   #**33**   Strategy

Power-Packed Postcards = Low-Cost Profits

Postcards are cost-effective tools for reaching your target audience. Most advertisers don't sell directly from postcards, but use them as lead-generating devices. You can mail them yourself, or if you're selling nationally, through co-op card pack decks. If you're interested in card decks (the ones containing 50 to 100 cards stacked and wrapped in cellophane), simply head for your local library and ask to see *The Standard Rates And Data Services* book (the "big red one"). Inside, you'll see hundreds of card decks that reach horizontal markets (all types of businesses) or specific vertical markets like accountants, printers, attorneys, etc.

If you're mailing the postcard yourself, you may want to create a double postcard format with a first class business reply card attached so that your prospects can mail back their responses. For maximum productivity, you can even create a postcard containing a reply card and your rolodex card for a three-in-one mailer! Just ask a printer about this.

Hint: Goldenrod (a deep yellow) is a proven, effective attention-getting color.

This bold copy pulls like a magnet! Notice how it follows the AIDA formula—Attention, Interest, Desire, Action. The free bonuses, no-obligation consultation and risk-reducing guarantee work together to "sweeten the pot."

My Copywriting Has Earned Millions For Others . . . Now Let Me Make Big Money For You.

Ace Ad Writer Dan McComas Guarantees Your Satisfaction Or His Work Is FREE!

How can I make such an amazing offer? By writing compelling cash-generating copy that motivates prospects to buy FASTER!

Experience pays: I increased the response to a previously written ad FIVE TIMES simply by changing the headline. I also just helped a bank rack up $33 million in home equity loan deposits, and a builder sell $2 million in homes with a modest $9K investment. Whether your business is large or small, chances are I can help you generate results just as remarkable!

Now, I can't predict the actual number of responses you'll receive, but I CAN guarantee results you're satisfied with . . . or my services are FREE! What's more, when you become my client, you'll receive a FREE consultation valued at $160. Just complete the other side, return it, and I'll do the rest. But hurry, my client roster is nearly full!

ADDED BONUS: Call My Marketing Hotline -- (301) 946-4284 -- and I'll help you improve the marketing document you're currently working on at NO CHARGE!

Call My Marketing Hotline Now -- (301) 946-4284 -- For FREE Marketing Advice!

Explosive, High-Profit Ads • Sales Letters • Flyers • Brochures and Publicity To Get You More Business NOW! Eye-Stopping Graphic Design Services Available Too!

YES! I want to know more about your copywriting services . . . especially your incredible offer to guarantee my marketing results. Please send information to:
(attach business card if you wish)   JLSM 4/92

Name: _____

Title: _____

Company: _____

Type of Business: _____

Street: _____

City: _____

State:_____ Zip: _____

Phone:(_____) _____
                      (in case I have questions)
Fax:(_____) _____

Copyright © 1991 by Dan McComas

Place
Stamp
Here

Dan McComas
"Copywriting That Sells... *Fast!*"
11409 Catalina Terrace
Silver Spring, MD 20902

MARKETING BOOT CAMP

Success #**34** Strategy

Stationery That Sells

Let your stationery tell people how you can help them!

Here's another example of "marketing mindset"—or communicating your advantages every chance you get. Why not present your benefits and credentials, services, hours, etc., in more than just ads, sales letters and brochures. Let your stationery tell people how you can help them. In the following letterhead sample, notice the positioning line and specific problem-solving information. You may also want to include professional credentials and affiliations and/or flexible payment plans. Hardly anyone does this. But now you'll want to consider creating benefit-oriented stationery next time you reprint your letterhead, you marketing maven.

THE INTERNATIONAL MARKETING INSTITUTE

Direct Response Marketing That Sells . . . Fast

11409 CATALINA TERRACE/SILVER SPRING, MD 20902/PHONE: 301-946-4284/FAX: 301-946-4104

High-Profit MARKETING Tools And TACTICS To BOOST YOUR REVENUES

Copywriting/Graphic Design
• MAGAZINE & NEWSPAPER ADS • BROCHURES • SALES LETTERS • FLYERS • DIRECT MAIL • PUBLICITY CONSULTATION

Speaking/Training
• MARKETING BOOT CAMPS • SELF-PROMOTION • NETWORKING • POWER WRITING • CREATIVITY • PRESENTATION SKILLS

Consulting Resources
• FREE INITIAL CONSULTATION • SECOND OPINION COPYWRITING CRITIQUES • MARKETING AUDITS
• MARKETING RESEARCH • ONE-ON-ONE MARKETING MENTOR PROGRAMS
• MONEY-MAKING BOOKS, TAPES & SPECIAL REPORTS

MARKETING BOOT CAMP

Success   #**35**   Strategy

Use Your Business Card As A Mini-Brochure

Take a moment now and look at the business cards you've collected at recent chamber meetings or networking events. Here's the problem. You can't remember what most of these individuals or companies actually do! OK, someone says she's an accountant. But what **kind** of financial help does she provide? What specific problems does she solve? What kinds of opportunities can she create for you? Be sure your card tells people *exactly* what you can do for them in benefit-rich detail. For example, to create additional space, you can inexpensively design and print a fold-over business card to tell people the specific ways you can help them. You can also print your benefits on the reverse side of your card. We don't understand why, but 95% of companies and individuals simply don't do this. But because you're always looking for ways to market better, you're going to join the 5% who do. Many people will actually compliment you on your card, which will accomplish two productive marketing missions. You'll stand out from the crowd . . . and you'll be remembered. You *really* can pull extra double duty from your business card!

Caution: Be sure your new "benefits" business card is tastefully designed.

How To Capitalize On Your Calling Card

Give out as many as you can, but even more important get *their* business card . . . and then follow up with a phone call, letter or thank-you card. Some key elements to consider when developing your business card are:

1. **Name**—Your name should be prominent on the card. You want people to remember you.
2. **Logo**—Depending on your company, consider incorporating a logo. This can help you develop a corporate identity.
3. **Business Name**—If your company name does not tell what you do, make sure you have a "tag line" underneath that explains your services and benefits.
4. **Address and Phone**—Make sure area code is listed. If you work from home and don't want your address listed, consider a private mailing box company such as Mail Box Etc. (look in yellow pages under answering services) instead of a P.O. Box #. Many people have negative connotations of P.O. Box #'s.
5. **Color**—Two background colors that stand out as providing a perception of quality are light gray and off white (beige).
6. **Size and Weight**—Ask for a standard size. Some people get oversized cards, but the people who receive them are many times at a loss about what to do with them. A good weight is 70-pound card stock.
7. **Foldover**—By having a foldover business card, you, for all practical purposes, have a mini-brochure.
8. **Pictures**—If you decide to have your picture on your card, make sure it shows you accomplishing something. For example a Realtor may want to have his or her hand on a sign that says, "SOLD!"

DAN McCOMAS ASSOCIATES
DIRECT RESPONSE MARKETING, COPYWRITING & CONSULTING

J. Daniel McComas, President

11409 Catalina Terrace, Silver Spring, Maryland 20902
Telephone (301)946-4284   FAX (301)946-4104

Over, please...

CONSULTING · COPY/DESIGN · SEMINARS/WORKSHOPS

- ☐ We help individuals and organizations sell more products and services *faster* and for *less cost* by creating results-oriented ads, flyers, brochures, sales letters and publicity.

- ☐ We offer keynote speeches and interactive workshops on marketing and sales, personal achievement and career advancement to build staff expertise and boost effectiveness.

- ☐ We accelerate careers by offering the best money-making books, tapes, special reports and software available.

RP REAL PROPERTIES

Wilbur Mondie
President

Suite 728
1311 Delaware Ave., S.W.
Washington, D.C. 20024   (202) 488 3590

I specialize in listing Foreclosure Property and Foreclosure Consultation. Consultation fee $120/Hr. (50% discount available)

Come to my monthly seminar *"How to Buy Foreclosure Property + How to Stop Foreclosures"* at the Learning Annex. For dates, time, cost and to register, call 966-9606.

Get my book *"How to Make Unlimited Money in Foreclosures and Real Estate Tax Sales plus How to Stop Foreclosures"* $29.95 or Book and 2 Cassette Tapes with step-by-step instructions $49.95 at Trover Shop Book Stores 543-8006, 227 Pennsylvania Avenue. S.E. & 1031 Connecticut Avenue N.W., Washington, D.C.

MARKETING BOOT CAMP

Success   #**36**   Strategy

Make Your Rolodex Card Outstanding

Yes, computer databases are taking over the world, but we'll bet, like us, you have a trusty, dog-eared rolodex sitting on your desk that you refer to regularly. Therefore . . .

1. You need a rolodex card.
2. You need a rolodex card that **stands out** from the pack with an extended color tab either on the right, middle or left side.
3. You should use a color stock or a second color.
4. You should create more than one rolodex card if you provide several services. Our friend Al Wood, a management and marketing consultant/trainer, does a nice job of touching all of the bases for the various services he provides. He has three, two-sided Rolodex cards: Speaker/Sales & Marketing, Management Institute/Management Consultant, Planning/Consultant.
5. You should be seen in the alphabetical listing of the service you provide regardless of the name of your business. "D" for Dermatologist, "O" for Office Supplies, "C" for Copywriter . . . you get the idea. And like on your business card, don't just list your services, be sure you telegraph your *benefits.*

MARKETING BOOT CAMP

Success #**37** Strategy

Gain Visibility, Build Credibility Through Free Publicity

It's been said that advertising is what you pay for, publicity is what you pray for. To have your prayers answered, you must think of PR not just as a press release, but as a *process* that helps you educate, inform and persuade your target audiences. That, dear reader, requires patient relationship building with the media. Like your targeted customer prospects, these journalists must get to know and trust you before you become an information or quotable resource. Give the media what they want and, in all likelihood, you'll get the consistent exposure you want and need to grow your business. Better still, publicity costs less and provides more credibility than you could ever achieve with paid advertising.

Get Your Share of The "Free" Publicity Pie

What do newspapers, magazines, trade publications, newsletters editors and television and radio producers want? They're hungry for news, "how to" articles, new services, new product releases and human interest stories to keep their readers and listeners informed and entertained. Eighty percent of the stories you see and hear every day in the print and electronic media have been provided or "planted" by companies and PR firms who know how to work with the appropriate media.

And you don't have to focus exclusively on newspapers. Industry or trade magazines and newsletters need your ideas, and, depending on your product or service, may deliver a more receptive audience for you than a general media outlet.

Positive publicity is one of the most powerful ways to reach, influence and motivate your prospects and customers to trust that your product or service can help them. That's because people tend to believe what they see and hear in the media. It's always more credible to have a third party say good things about you than to blow your own horn. Think of "the media" not so much as a group, but as individual editors, reporters and broadcasters with one purpose: to educate, entertain and offer news to their readers, listeners and viewers. If you can help them accomplish this while making it **easy** for them to use your information, they'll consistently look to you as a resource.

The media are interested in many types of communications from your company. Here's a sampling of the subjects you can offer to establish yourself as a valuable resource:

- Company, individual or product success stories
- Case histories of successful services and products/how people are using them
- New products or services
- Executive appointments, promotions
- New clients
- Research/industry forecasts and trends
- Survey results
- Community involvement
- Trade shows

One-on-one meetings and editorial tours of your company with local and regional editors are excellent ways to build relationships with the media. Another effective tool for businesses working with industry publications is to create and submit a camera-ready feature story. You'd be surprised how many periodicals will pick up a well-written, ready-to-go article. Why? It offers news or value to their readers and it's incredibly **easy** for the editor to use!

Hint: Especially with new-product introductions, it's a good idea to include the cost and how and where to get it.

Following are general tips for working effectively with reporters and editors:

1. **Keep an updated press file in your database similar to your prospect/customer file.** Change is a constant for media people, so you must stay on top of this. Be sure to target "influencer" publication/stations and a list of journalists with whom you can establish in-depth relationships.

2. **Find a hook, an angle or unusual twist to your story.** "Man Bites Dog" always gets more press or air time than "Dog Bites Man." Use the creativity techniques we recommend in this book (see #47) to brainstorm unique approaches.

3. **Timing is everything.** Tie your story to a particular season, event, holiday, or national news story. A recent article in the business section of *The Washington Post* revealed that most Americans are in the dark about how to manage their money and investments. This is a perfect opportunity for a financial planner to run an ad saying: *"According To A Recent Survey Conducted By [the source], 9 Out Of 10 Americans Have Absolutely No Idea How To Manage Their Investments. Are You One Of Them?"* Then, in the ad, offer a free booklet titled *"10 Simple Strategies For Managing And Generating Higher Returns On Your Personal Investments"* and just wait for the phone to ring.

4. **Make your press release, how-to article or feature story factual.** There's a fine line to walk between facts and promo copy but one thing is certain: editors will "round file" anything that smacks of hype or extravagance. It's not their job to promote your company. Remember, you're not offering news or information to *them* per se, but to their readers and listeners.

5. **Meet deadlines.** Regrettably, many publicity opportunities are lost every day because an individual or company missed a media deadline. Be sure to ask each publication or station for its editorial calendar and deadlines. Also, when speaking to a reporter, your first question should be, "Are you on deadline?" If the answer is yes, quickly ask when you can return the call, thank the reporter and hang up. Many editors and reporters don't work 9 to 5 jobs, so you must be available day or night when they need a quote or have a question.

6. **Call editors with your story ideas.** Due to multiple deadline pressures, media people need "reminder" calls. Once you've submitted an article or news release you've discussed with an editor, feel free to call to see if he or she has received it and if there are any questions. Don't call to ask if they've "picked up" or used your release. That's a dead giveaway that you don't read their publication or listen to or watch their shows.

Continuous, positive press coverage provides you with the image of a winner in the eyes of your target audiences. And people like to work with winners.

Steps For Writing A Winning News Release

1. Write the release on your letterhead with the word "NEWS."

2. Depending upon your timing, include the date you would like your news released or say "For Immediate Release" if it can be used upon receipt.

3. Include your name or your contact's name and phone (office and home—reporters work around the clock; be available and sensitive to their deadlines).

4. Double-space your type so editors can make notes—avoid typos.

5. Put your most important information (what? who? when? where? how?) in the headline and lead paragraph. Editors cut from the bottom up.

6. Avoid adjectives and hype—this is not ad writing but "fact" writing. Be specific. Back it up with quotes and statistics whenever possible.

Type ### or —END— when finished.

James C. Smith & Associates
422 South Street • Suite 400 • Boulder, CO 80301

News

For immediate release
Contact: Peter Jamison
Day: 303-245-5566   Evening: 303-933-4478

LOCAL BUSINESS VALUATION FIRM ISSUES FREE SPECIAL REPORT

The office of James C. Smith & Associates, a business valuation specialist headquartered in Boulder, Colorado, has issued a special report entitled, "What is YOUR Business Worth?" James C. Smith & Associates is making copies of the report available free of charge to those who call its toll-free 24-hour business hotline number, 1-800-333-2525.

According to Peter Jamison, partner of JCS, the report is intended to serve ". . . closely held companies which can, overnight, find themselves confronting the need to learn just how much their business is worth."

"Emergencies happen every day," says Mr. Jamison. "An owner dies, or becomes permanently disabled. Long-standing partnership disagreements suddenly boil over into full-scale warfare, setting a buy-sell agreement into motion. Or a marriage breakup necessitates a sale. Sometimes, a business loses a major customer and the owner or owners have to get financing to tide them over. That means owners, or survivors, are suddenly faced with figuring out the worth of an enterprise while facing intense emotional stress—and none of us does our best work under these conditions. I hope this report will help business people in Boulder to attain some insights into the virtues of knowing what their businesses are worth today, so they can get more for them tomorrow," Mr. Jamison concluded.

James C. Smith & Associates provides independent, unbiased third-party business valuation services, including valuation support for buy/sell agreements, estate and gift taxes, mergers and acquisitions, recapitalizations/financing litigation support and intangible assets. The company is located in downtown Boulder.

####

Free Publicity . . . Your Best Publicity

Radio and television stations, newspapers and magazines are always looking for guests. Every day thousands of guests are needed throughout the United States. And they are looking for entrepreneurs and executives like you! The reason free publicity on radio, television and in print works better than paid advertisements is the credibility factor. When someone sees or hears you on a talk show or reads about you in print, their perception is that your company must know its business. To help you get booked on radio and television shows, or to get your articles published, you'll want to investigate the following resources. The first three may either be purchased or located in your local library.

Here's an effective resource to help you identify and contact 1,591 daily newspapers, 13,848 weekly newspapers and 9,677 trade/consumer magazines and newsletters.

Bacon's Publicity Checker
Bacon's Publishing Company
332 S. Michigan Avenue
Chicago, IL 60604
(312) 922-2400

Bacon's also publishes lists for radio and television stations.

For listings of 1,627, daily and 5,867 weekly newspapers, 235 magazines, 430 trade magazines, 2,820 professional business publications and many radio and television stations, you will also want to consider:

All-in-One Directory
Gebbie Press, Inc.
P.O. Box 1000
New Paltz, NY 12561
(914) 255-7560

Over 20,000 specialized newsletter publishers are eager to hear from you too. One of the best resources for identifying and contacting the publications that target your audiences is:

Oxbridge Dictionary of Newsletters
Oxbridge Communications
150 5th Avenue, Suite 302
New York, NY 10011
(212) 741-0231

Products need publicity, and publications need products to publicize. The publicity is free, it's just a matter of targeting product releases to the appropriate publications—and in formats that editors can use. For your press release planning, you'll want to see *Marketing Made Easier, Guide To Free Publicity* by Barry Klein (Todd Publications). All the information has been organized to provide you with valuable shortcuts to finding the print sources that match your product or publicity needs. The directory is divided into two parts: alphabetical—with listings of more than 1,000 magazines, newsletters and trade publications; and by target index—containing approximately 120 target audiences matched to specific publications serving that particular audience. This handy guide is $25. Call (301) 946-4284 for details.

Selling Information Products via Nationwide Talk Radio. If you have a book or information product to sell and are looking for a low-cost publicity strategy for promoting it, you may want to contact our friend Joe Sabah. Joe and his wife Judy self-publish a book titled *How To Get The Job You Really Want And Get Employers To Call You*. They've sold over 19,000 copies almost exclusively through national talk radio programs from home/office telephone interviews and Joe has created a step-by-step system and a list of stations to help anyone do this. You can reach him at Pacesetter Publications, P.O. Box 101330, Denver, CO 80250, (303) 722-7200.

The *United Way Media Fact Book.* For about $10 this book lists every TV, radio station, newspaper and magazine in most cities. Just give the United Way in your area a call.

The *Directory of Experts, Authorities and Spokespersons.* For a small fee you can put your ad into this directory. It's distributed to almost every television station, radio station, magazine and newspaper throughout the USA. When someone needs a guest, there's a good chance they'll look up someone like you. For more information call the publisher, Mitch Davis, at (202) 333-4904.

Send Your News Release via Fax. Instead of licking stamps you can have Business Wire, (212) 575-8822, or PR Newswire, (212) 832-9400), reach over 2,000 print and broadcast editions in minutes at reasonable costs.

MARKETING BOOT CAMP

Success #**38** Strategy

Write . . . Write . . . Write—
Get Published Now!

Many of the marketing successes we've enjoyed have come from potential clients reading articles we've written or been interviewed in or from our books. Getting published establishes credibility you just can't get from paid advertising. When people read about you in an article or see one you've written, their perception is that "this person must be good. After all, not just anyone could be in this publication."

For example, a recent article Arnold wrote on communication skills for a local Washington, DC publication provided him with 11 speaking engagements. In addition to the impact a published article can make, the reprints are worth their weight in gold. When a potential client wants more information, we bring along or mail reprints of our articles. In many cases this is the only promotional material we need to close a deal. Besides using the *United Way Media Fact Book* and the *Directory of Experts, Authorities and Spokespersons*, we also recommend you look at the *Writers Market* for magazine contacts (located in book stores). In many cases we advise our clients to call local magazines and newspapers and let them know they are available for an interview, or to write a story on a topic that would be of interest to their audiences. For example, Todd Taskey, a Financial Planner with Solutions Planning Group in Bethesda, Maryland, made a cold call to the *Washington Business Journal* to tell them that an interview or profile of him would be of interest to their readers. The writer agreed and within a short time they published an article on him. Besides the great response he received, he now has a reprint to send to clients and potential clients.

Washington
BUSINESS JOURNAL

VOLUME 12, NUMBER 25   WHERE WASHINGTON CAPITALIZES ON BUSINESS   WEEK NOVEMBER 5-11, 1993

Solutions to financial planning, personal wealth

PHOTO BY JOANNE S LAWTON

Todd R. Taskey: Providing personal wealth strategies.

By JO GORDON

Company: SOLUTIONS PLANNING GROUP INC.

Business address: 3 Metro Center, #900, Bethesda, Md. 20814   301-951-5544

President: TODD R. TASKEY, CFP

Taskey began his career in financial services in 1987 as a life insurance salesman. After realizing that "life insurance was not the perfect investment for all of the people all of the time," he began to learn the investment planning business.

Taskey earned his degree as a Certified Financial Planner and then as a Certified Fund Specialist and began providing investment planning services primarily to business professionals using non-commission mutual funds in order to provide top management and non-biased advice.

Today, Taskey is well recognized in the financial planning industry. He has hosted his own financial radio program, teaches financial planning for Montgomery College, appears regularly in the financial press and is a frequent guest on radio programs across the country.

Greatest challenge: Solutions was faced with a constantly and dynamically changing investment and tax environment. Educating clients to be patient in the long term was a challenge.

"To provide the level of investment performance and service that clients need in order to succeed was very challenging," Taskey says. "You have to be extremely knowledgeable." His certification as a fund specialist and financial planner helped. Knowing the tax law "inside and out" was also useful.

"The way we operate helped us get past the obstacles. We don't represent insurance companies or mutual fund companies — we represent our clients. This philosophy helped us to weather many a storm. Our clients appreciate the different slant we have," says Taskey.

Today, Solutions' clients are drawn primarily from referrals. Taskey says he rarely advertises.

Number of employees: Solutions has three full-time employees. The majority of investment and tax planning research is done by outside firms and mutual fund analysts.

Sales: In the financial planning industry,

"sales" are more accurately measured by clients and assets under management.

Solutions' clientele has grown by an average of 34 percent over the past four years, while assets under management have increased eightfold since 1989. 1993-1994 should see assets under management double again, Taskey projects. In 1989, assets under management totaled around $250,000. The figure for 1993 is expected to be close to the $3-million mark.

On average, Solutions brings in around $62,000 in monthly contributions for clients.

Description of business: Solutions was started and incorporated in 1989 when Taskey "kind of fell into this business" after finishing school.

"We help clients plan their financial and investment lives by considering tax planning, insurance and investment strategies. We do it differently. We don't sell financial products. We sell financial management planning. If you were sick, you wouldn't call on a drug rep. You'd want an unbiased opinion. That's what we offer."

Solutions' clients are both individual business people and businesses, primarily in Washington, D.C. Many of the former, says Taskey, are attorneys and physicians. He says heads of small businesses have the most difficulty in the area of financial planning because they're at the helm of their companies, charged with a whole host of responsibilities. On top of everything, they have to figure out the best way to deal with retirement planning.

"Through the use of favorable tax strategies, proper investment planning, and thorough insurance planning, the consistent growth of personal wealth is inevitable for our clients," Taskey says.

Best advice: "If you do not doubt in your mind but believe in your heart, all things are possible to you." — Mark 11:24.

Reprinted with permission from the Washington Business Journal.

Also, if you have the fortitude for it, take the time to write a book. There are many conventional publishers and you may or may not get published. If you want to move quickly, we suggest that you consider self-publishing. Many best sellers were at first self-published. When sales started going well the rights were then sold to a publisher. The main advantage of writing a book is the credibility you'll receive and the increased list of customers that will come to you. Arnold, who wrote *"You Can Start Your Own Business,"* does not have to prove himself when he meets potential customers. People immediately think, "He must know what he's doing, after all he's the one who wrote the book." Besides the credibility, Arnold uses copies of his book as a calling card. Instead of giving people a brochure, he lets the book speak for him. One great resource to help you get your book published is Kendall/Hunt Publishing Company. You can reach them by calling David Metcalf at (703) 237-1907.

How To Write A Business "How To" Article . . . And Get It Published

People are hungry for information. Why? They want to solve their problems or improve their lot. That means editors and reporters are always looking for advice that informs and entertains their readers. What you must do is convince the editor that your article will meet these requirements. And with so many newspapers, magazines, business publications and industry newsletters, it's not difficult. What do you write about? For our purposes, let's assume you've never done this before.

1. **The Topic.** Select a topic that offers helpful advice or information. A plumber could title an article, *"The Easiest Way To Install A New Sink."* An accountant might write about *"5 Tips To Help You Pay Hundreds—Even Thousands Less To Uncle Sam."* Look at the headline samples in this book (#23) to jump-start your thinking. The point is to provide enough (but not too much) information to assist people with the task at hand and, more importantly, to be perceived as a helpful or specialized problem-solver. If you're at a loss for a topic or background material, gather your company or industry's current marketing materials. Chances are you can adapt or structure your message around that copy.

2. **The Length.** Before you begin writing you must know the length and types of articles used by the publication. Most "how to" articles are 250, 500, 1,000 or 2,500 words.

3. **Use a Numbered Sequence.** The easiest, fastest way to write a "how to" article is with a numbered sequence structure like "10 Ways To," "The 5 Inside Secrets Of ___," "25 Ways To Improve Customer Service," etc.

4. **Start Writing and Keep Writing.** Remember, there's a BIG difference between writing and editing. Don't try to edit as you write. Well, it's true. Why? Because that little negative voice inside your head will start saying things like, "What? Who are *you* to write an article?", or "You see, I *knew* you couldn't write, just look at that grammar"—or "Hey, your spelling's atrocious!" The best way to defeat these mental blocks (which reside in all of us to one degree or another) is to Write. Write. Write. Don't stop until you've exhausted your ideas. Even if you run out of ideas **keep your fingers moving on the keyboard** and type something like—hdriertnasdsfiee blah-blah-dum-te-dum—adherfvnfkjiri—until more ideas surface. And they will! Now . . . read it over. Don't worry about grammar, structure, logical sequence or spelling. You can take care of that in the editing stage. Finally, walk away from it for a day and let your unconscious mind (the most creative part) take over. During the next 24 hours you'll come up with even more ideas and better ways to communicate them. You'll want to have a tape recorder or note pad by your bed to capture these inspirations—some will be brilliant and some laughable. Now incorporate this additional information, look at your article with fresh eyes and begin editing and polishing. In some paragraphs you'll be making wholesale changes, in others it will just be a matter of fine-tuning. Perhaps you've heard the truism that writing is 1% inspiration and 99% perspiration.

5. **Use a Photo.** Remember to include a 5" x 7" glossy black and white photo "head-shot" when you send off your article. Most publications will use them, some will not.

6. **Congratulations. You're an Author!** Feels great doesn't it?
   Hint: You may want to try this time-saving technique: Some writers find that dictating their article into a tape recorder and then transcribing the material is an efficient way to work.

Caution: Never create an article that reads like a commercial for you or your company. Your target audience will never see it because the editor will never print it.

Convincing The Media To Publish Your Article

There are several strategies for approaching a reporter or editor. The fastest way is to phone first and present your article idea. Editors are busy so be sure to immediately explain how it will help their readers. Another way is to mail a query letter (with or without your article) and follow-up with a phone call. Also, you should get ahold of that publication's editorial calendar to tie your future articles to seasonal or special theme editions.

In most cases, you won't get paid for these articles. But that's not your intention. You see, you're going to request that the publication run your biography or resource box at the end of the article. What's a biography box? It's a mini-advertisement about you and your problem-solving expertise which provides a vehicle for your readers to connect with you. It might say "Jim Smith is a CPA and partner in the firm of Smith, Lambert and Jenkins based in Charlottesville, VA. His firm specializes in saving small business owners money on their taxes. For a free copy of his *"Business Owners: Never Pay More Than You Have To"* kit, call Jim at (804) 992-5780. Now your readers have a reason to connect with you. Trade publications and newsletters will typically run your bio box as you present it, however most newspapers will only run your name, title, company name and city. Oh yes, remember to put © 1994 by Jim Smith at the bottom of your article to automatically copyright your work.

Yes, people will read your by-lined article and compliment you and it will feel good. You'll also get calls that may result in new business. But the largest leverage you'll receive is by photocopying or reprinting your article and mailing it to your prospects and clients with a handwritten note that says, "Thought you'd be interested in my recently published article on how to [whatever your article was about]." You can also bind the article into proposals and use it as a handout at speaking engagements or civic, association and chamber meetings. It's a powerful business building tool that you can keep in your company's marketing arsenal and your personal propaganda package for years.

Note: If you don't have the time or inclination to write an article yourself, you can call in a business freelance writer to ghostwrite it for you. Simply have him or her interview you over the phone or in person. Don't fret over this method. After all, they're *your* ideas and many busy people do this. Just call your local Chamber of Commerce for a referral, place an ad in the paper, or look under "copywriter" or "writer" in your phone book. Congratulations! Now that you have your article in hand . . . go out and spread the profitable news!

Here is a sample query letter you can adapt for your purposes.

Dear [Editor's Name]:

Small businesses are paying more taxes than they have to. Every day we help our clients (many of them your readers), save hundreds or even thousands of dollars simply by making small adjustments in their accounting procedures.

That's why I wrote *"5 Little Known Accounting Secrets That Can Save Your Business Hundreds—Even Thousands of Dollars Every Year."*

The 500 word article is enclosed for your review. (Or I have an article idea that . . .) I believe it would be of great interest and benefit to your readers during the busy tax months of February and March.

I will call you shortly to gauge your interest.

Sincerely,

Jim Smith, CPA

P.S. By way of introduction, I've owned my CPA firm for 12 years. I have over 1,500 clients and four associates working with me.

Here's a "how to" business article. Notice the resource box in the lower left hand corner.

Writing Copy That Sells

by Dan McComas

Your company is ready to introduce a new product or service and it is up to you, the company's jack-of-all-marketing, public relations and advertising functions, to write the promotional materials. The kind of persuasive materials that will consistently stuff your mailbox with leads and checks and make your phone ring off the hook.

Facing the Dilemma Head On

After the anxiety eases, you realize you have a dilemma. Should you rearrange your four-page "to-do" list and make this the top priority, or do you hire a professional copywriter? If you are lucky enough to find money in the budget for a copywriter, it is still up to you to manage the project. This means knowing that this expert should include the following six elements in your copy.

1 What's In It For Me?
You have only two to three seconds to immediately address the prospect's self-interest—how your service or product will improve the prospect's comfort, pleasure, profit or status. Weak writing explains only the features of a service or product. Strong writing turns features into specific benefits.

2 Action Words.
Make sure your copy contains persuasive "power" words like: You. New. Free. Introducing. Save. Discount. First Time Ever. Discover. Love. Instantly. Proven. Easy. Offer. Guaranteed. Now. Remarkable. Incredible. Secret. Attention. Announcing. Last Chance. At Last.

3 Compelling Look and Sound.
The copy should be written in a simple, conversational style at an eighth-grade level. This means using short sentences, short paragraphs, contractions and lots of "you's." Put passion in your copy and avoid industry jargon at all costs. The copy's visual approach should include benefit-rich headlines and subheads, as well as eye-catching graphics such as bullets, boxes, underlines, arrows, boldface type, etc.

3 Confidence and Believability.
It's natural for prospects to be wary of your offers and promises. Your copy must instill confidence by providing specific evidence that your product or service will do what you say it will. You have to make the decision painless by including "risk reducers" like solid guarantees, surveys, case studies or problems you solved and client testimonials.

And never underestimate the power of emotion-based selling. Most people buy with their hearts (emotion) and rationalize decisions with their heads (logic). Success stories and facts provide the evidence of the emotional advantages or benefits you have promised and the logical "reasons why" and excuses for buying.

5 Elicit A Response Now.
To get your prospects to act on your offer sooner rather than later be sure your copy includes these interactive marketing techniques:
- ask prospects to write, phone, or request free literature;
- offer a free consultation or seminar program;
- include a hot-line number;
- take credit cards;
- ask for a return coupon and/or check;

6 Create A Sense of Urgency.
Does the copy compellingly communicate what your prospects will lose if they don't act now? To get them to connect with you faster, your copy should include limited time offers, limited supply declarations, early-bird specials, and two-for-one offers.

Taking the Most Direct Route

Many people think of a marketing and advertising campaign as a hit or miss proposition. And when it misses, many chalk it up to the fault of the product or service. In reality, the right marketing or advertising copy can make a difference in your bottom line.

Effective copy tells your prospects exactly what to do and makes it easy for them to reply or order. Be specific. **Don't just hint. Getting them to act now is your primary objective.**

> Put passion in your copy and avoid industry jargon at all costs.

Dan McComas is a direct response copywriter and speaker. Some of his work includes creating brochures, ads, sales letters and public relations consultations. He is currently President of Dan McComas Associates and can be reached at 301.946.4284.

WBA | 3

Reprinted with permission from the Washington Business Advisor.

MARKETING BOOT CAMP

Success #**39** Strategy

Networking . . . What Is It?

Finding a good networker is like finding a good friend; they are few and far between. The main principle behind networking is sharing. Unfortunately, too many people take, take, take and never give back. We define networking as the providing of leads, contacts, information and ideas for the mutual benefit of you and the people in your network. According to Anthony Putman, author of *"Marketing Your Services,"* the purpose of networking is to give and get information. If you network properly, nobody feels pressured or used. You are not selling, you are telling. You are not asking for favors, you are giving valuable information.

Everyone networks. To be a successful networker you must first look at how effective your networking has been up to now. By reflecting where you've been, you can then set the gears in motion to develop a focused networking approach versus an arbitrary one. To see how effective your networking has been, ask yourself the following questions.

1. Why do you network?
2. When do you network?
3. How do you network?
4. Whom do you network with?
5. What strategies do you use to network?
6. Do your networking exchanges end up in a Win-Win situation?
7. Which network opportunities are the most and least productive?

MARKETING BOOT CAMP

Success **#40** Strategy

Networking . . . Where To Start?

1. **Set networking goals.** An important part of your marketing strategy is to make networking a *planned* activity versus an arbitrary tool that you practice now and then. In developing networking goals, you should determine the types of people you want to meet, how many you want to meet, and what functions you are going to attend.

2. **Be specific.** While networking, be very specific about the *type* of person you want to meet. How many times have you heard or asked this question: "Do you know anyone who could use my services?" The answer is typically "Let me think about it."

   To make sure this doesn't happen to you, let everyone know the exact title of the person you wish to connect with. For example, the people who hire speakers and trainers (like us) look for Training Directors, Meeting Planners, Human Resources Directors, Personnel Directors, Association Directors and high level company personnel. Whenever you have the opportunity to meet someone or when introducing yourself at networking sessions, be reading ready with your *"16-Second Sizzler"*—your personal or company benefit statement. This technique makes it easy for people to understand and remember exactly what you do. Here's Arnold's "16-Second Sizzler":

   The Business Source is a business development and training company. We focus on designing and presenting seminars and workshops to help individuals and organizations increase sales and cut costs. Additionally, we offer consulting services on marketing, presentation skills and customer service.

3. **Work with your current network.** Review your rolodex file, your address book, your business card file, phone index and correspondence files. Even if some of these people are not your target market, they know others who are. Organize your contacts by category and place them in separate files. In addition, there are two contact management software programs we can recommend— **Ascend** and **Act.** Both can be found at almost any computer software store.

4. **Get involved.** Go to meetings of the rotary club and other civic and fraternal organizations, church groups, trade and professional groups and self help groups such as toastmasters; teach adult education classes in your community or for the local community college or university; join the local chamber of commerce; and more. In addition there are many networking "lead" or "tipster" clubs you can join or create yourself.

5. **Increase your visibility.** Speak before groups at every opportunity you can, write articles for trade publications or newsletters or become an officer in your club. All these add to your credibility and motivate people to seek *you* out!

6. **Make contacts.** Whether it's a business or social situation and you want to meet someone, just do it. Take the risk, what do you have to lose? The more people you know, the more opportunities will come your way.

7. **Don't hustle.** The bottom line behind marketing is to make friends. Don't push yourself on others. Effective networking takes time. Find out what you have in common and how you can help each other. The best way to start off with someone new in your network is for you to ask, "What can I do to help you?"

8. **Ask.** If you don't ask for what you want, you won't get it. Find the person who can help you . . . and whom you can help. Then ask.

9. **Recommend others.** Always recommend and promote others in your network. For example, many times people come to us with a service or product need that we can't fulfill. Instead of saying we can't handle it, we try to match them with clients and suppliers in our network. It's great extra value to your client when you can recommend them to someone. Imagine how loyal that client will be! To help you in this process we recommend that you keep a file in your computer called "Peoples' Needs." Make a list of what people are looking for—then, when someone calls that you can't personally help, you'll have quick access to people you can recommend.

10. **Keep in touch.** Ever hear the saying, "What have you done for me lately?" People forget about you *very quickly* unless you keep in touch. We recommend staying in contact with clients and those in your network at least once every two months. For example, you can send articles that are relevant to them (even better—send articles you have written!), call them to see how they are coming along, ask them to lunch, play golf, send them a copy of your newsletter and so on. Whatever you do—stay in touch!

11. **Network with competitors.** Twenty percent of our business comes from our competitors. By developing a trusting relationship, it's amazing how you can help each other. For example, we sometimes decline certain jobs because we don't have the time or inclination. By referring it to our competitor, everybody wins. The client gets the service he or she wants, the competitor gets the work, and we get goodwill and a referral fee from our competitor. Also, the competitors we work with understand that this is *our* client and any request for future work must come through us first.

12. **The more you give, the more you get.** When someone gives you a lead, referral, new business or an idea, make a special effort to return the favor as quickly as you can. In addition, make sure you always send a handwritten thank-you to show your appreciation.

MARKETING BOOT CAMP

Success   #**41**   Strategy

Networking . . . Where To Go?

Wherever there is another human being there is an opportunity to network. Did you know that the average person has 250 contacts or more and that you are only four or five people away from virtually anyone you want to meet? In fact, we mentioned this very point at a recent seminar and a woman came up to us after the event to tell us she was friends with the Vice President's family. Moments later she said she would recommend our company to conduct training seminars at The White House!

Whether you're at a party, on a plane, waiting in line for groceries or any other place where you see people, the opportunities for business are there. In addition to "running into people," we would like to recommend three proven networking strategies:

1. **Business Card Mixers**—These are sponsored by chambers of commerce throughout the United States and Canada. The events are usually free, though some may charge a small fee. In most cases you don't have to be a member and the advantage is that everyone expects you to exchange leads with them in a nonthreatening environment. Mixers generally take place right after work and are usually sponsored and held in a member's office. Their primary purpose is for people to get acquainted and help each other with leads, ideas and information. A client of ours gets all his business from these events. In fact, he averages about 12 appointments from each meeting!

2. **Rolodex Parties**—This consists of meeting with another person who may have potential clients for you and you for him or her. For example, both individuals should bring their rolodexes of past clients, contacts, friends, etc., then take turns on the phone calling

on behalf of the other person. This works well because if a client likes and trusts us and we recommend the other person, that trust is transferred. Just be sure you have confidence in the person you're recommending.

3. **Networking Clubs**—Join an established club or develop one of your own. Networking clubs provide a structured environment for people to share leads, information and ideas. By meeting on a regular basis and getting to know the people in the club, you become a team where everyone is consciously working to help each other. It's almost like having 15 associates as personal marketing agents. To develop a club of your own, start with another person. For the first meeting each of you is responsible for bringing someone from a different business. You continue to do this until you have between 10 to 20 people. The club usually meets once a week for one hour. Everyone goes around the room and explains who they are, what they do, and the kinds of opportunities they're looking for. After each person has had a turn, they go around the room and explore the contacts and information they have to help each other. To minimize competition for the leads, you only want one person from each discipline or industry. In addition to forming your own club there are opportunities through associations, professional and trade organizations, fraternal, church, school groups and others.

MARKETING BOOT CAMP

Success   #**42**   Strategy

Networking . . . What To Say?

Many business people squander networking opportunities by incessantly talking about themselves. Successful networking requires that you get out of *your* mind and into the mind of the person you're talking to by asking the right questions. The following queries can lead you to what you want.

1. Can you introduce me to __?
2. Who else should I read, go, do, __?
3. Who has made a difference in your life lately __?
4. How else can I assist you __?
5. What do you recommend regarding __? (i.e., getting clients)
6. What insiders' report or newsletters do you receive __?
7. Who else should I meet __?
8. How can we take what we've done and use it again __?
9. What do I need to do to make something happen __?
10. Who makes the decisions __?

To be a good networker . . . be a good conversationalist

Is your voice always a monotone or do you speak enthusiastically?
Are you self-centered or other-oriented?
Do you try to dominate conversations?
Do you talk too much, over explain or lecture others?
Are you a complainer?
Do you talk to people about things they're interested in?
Do you smile, laugh easily and respond to others genuinely?
Can you discuss subjects besides your job or home life?
Do you get to the point quickly or do you go into excruciating detail?
Are you open, candid, direct and friendly?
Do you have good eye contact?
Are you an active and sympathetic listener?
Do you ask others open ended questions that draw them out?
Do you ask others about how they feel about a subject?

MARKETING BOOT CAMP

Success #**43** Strategy

Direct Mail . . . Your Checklist

Ask yourself these questions before your mail goes out the door:

1. Do you look at the mail as the reader would?
2. Do you keep your primary objective in mind?
3. Does the #1 benefit instantly hit you between the eyes?
4. Does your message flow?
5. Does the outside envelope encourage you to open it *now*?
6. Is the letter the first thing you see upon opening?
7. Does the letter or flyer point out the reader's needs, product benefits, features, endorsement and how to respond?
8. Do the graphics support the copy?
9. Does the reply card explain the entire offer?
10. Is there a reason to act now . . . is it easy to respond?
11. Would you respond to the package?

Direct mail consists of sending sales materials to potential customers. The materials can be either flyers, letters, brochures, coupons or other specially designed materials. Direct mail can either be your least or most expensive marketing strategy. To make sure your direct mail piece is effective in both cost and results, ask the questions above and remember the three steps to a great mail piece.

1. **You must target the right audience**—Are you sending materials to the most qualified potential customers?

2. **You must make the right offer**—What incentives can you offer to get them to want to purchase your product or service now?

3. **You must package the materials so they will open it**—Make sure your mail package has incentives on it so they will open it!

MARKETING BOOT CAMP

Success   #**44**   Strategy

How To Purchase A Mailing List

A mailing list can be a great bargain or a very expensive mistake. In most cases you'll be renting a list for one-time use only. You can purchase lists for unlimited usage, but the cost is usually steep. We suggest you ask the following questions to the mailing list broker before your purchase.

- ➪ Is the owner's list compatible with your products or services?
- ➪ How old is the list—when were the names acquired?
- ➪ Who else has rented the list—what did they offer?
- ➪ How were the names originally obtained?
- ➪ What price did the list owner charge for the product or service?
- ➪ How often has the list been rented in the last year . . . is it over-used?
- ➪ When was the list cleaned (checked for dates, name and address changes)?
- ➪ Are the demographics (age, sex, income, region) of the list comparable to yours?
- ➪ What is your gut feeling about the list?

Mailing list brokers can be found in the *Standard Rate and Data Services* (SRDS) book at your main library. Here are two you may wish to contact for infomation or list catalogs:

Dunhill of Washington
(202) 331-7724

R.L. Polk & Co.
(313) 292-3200

MARKETING BOOT CAMP
Success #**45** Strategy

Pay $$$ For Qualified Leads . . .
Give Referral Fees

One of the best ways to get new business is to offer referral fees. By offering people generous incentives, you'll get plenty of business. Also, if
you do get a qualified referral, make sure you pay the referrer immediately. We like to pay referrers in cash so they really get excited about
finding us more work! Here's a flyer Arnold uses to consistently generate attention and results for his speaking business! (P.S. The offer on the
flyer is still good.)

To make sure your referral fee program works, follow these guidelines:

⇨ Pay referrers immediately. Don't make them wait, and above all,
   don't make them chase you down to get their referral fee.
⇨ Let referrers know that if any other business comes from the
   client they referred, you will give them a referral fee for the
   next year.
⇨ We give fees ranging from 10% to 20% and more. Make the
   incentive so great that they'll be looking for you all the time.
⇨ Put the referral flyer on bulletin boards, car windows, leave at
   events, as inserts in newsletters and at seminars where you
   speak.

MARKETING BOOT CAMP

Success #**46** Strategy

Speak Out For More Business

Speaking will help you gain both visibility and credibility. Fortunately for you (and us) very few people even consider speaking to build their businesses. According to *Book of Lists,* the number one fear of Americans is speaking before a group. In fact, *dying* is number six on the list!

That means you have a golden opportunity to speak before and influence the members of groups in Rotary clubs, chambers of commerce, Lion's clubs, civic groups, business and trade organizations, political affiliations, church groups and countless others who are *always* looking for interesting speakers.

We've spoken at numerous luncheons and dinners and have received more solid contacts and profitable opportunities than we could ever get cold calling. You can also offer to teach a class for your local adult education center, or the continuing education departments of your local university. You'll enjoy instant credibility, and education directors will refer you to people who call in looking for someone with your expertise. Also, your class and biography will be advertised under the institution's name and sent to thousands of households. How's that for free advertising! Another speaking strategy is to design and offer a public seminar. However, self-sponsored, for-profit seminars can be risky for beginners as well as veteran speakers.

The more professional the presentation by you and/or your associates, the greater chance you'll have of persuading potential clients to try your services. The two most critical aspects of successful presentations are planning and delivery. Ninety percent of the success of a presentation can be attributed to planning. To develop a successful blueprint you need to answer the following questions:

- ⮕ Who are your participants? Do they share the same experiences?
- ⮕ Do the participants have the knowledge or skills that pertain to the topic?
- ⮕ What is their education level?
- ⮕ How many participants will attend the presentation?
- ⮕ What is the preferred learning style of the group (i.e., lectures, demonstrations)?
- ⮕ How much time will you have for the presentation?
- ⮕ How will you get and keep their attention?
- ⮕ What questions will you ask? What questions will they ask?
- ⮕ What notes, visuals and materials will you need?

To make your presentation a winner, follow these guidelines:

- ⮕ Be sure to tell your audience why your presentation is relevant to them.
- ⮕ Keep your presentation within or under the allotted time.
- ⮕ Make sure you have enough breaks. Research shows that adult concentration plummets after 1 hour and 15 minutes.
- ⮕ Don't tell jokes unless you are a great storyteller . . . and then make certain your story isn't offensive.
- ⮕ Eliminate all material not directly relevant to the central theme of your presentation.
- ⮕ Make sure your visual aids are not crutches. Do not overwhelm your audience with them.
- ⮕ Maintain eye contact with your audience throughout your presentation.
- ⮕ Listen actively to audience questions. Always rephrase the question before you respond.
- ⮕ Stay with topics you really care about. That way, your enthusiasm will shine through. People are more convinced by the enthusiasm of your message than by the message itself.

↪ Be authentic. Use your own unique presentation style. To come across as genuine, sincere and knowledgeable, you must be yourself.

↪ Use this time-proven structure for a speech: "Tell them what you're going to tell them. Tell them. Tell them what you've told them."

↪ Keep the audience's attention. Have a question, anecdote, story, exercise or discussion point every three to five minutes.

↪ Have an attention-getting opener by asking a question, sharing a personal experience or anecdote, starting with a strong statistic, commenting on a current event or using a visual.

↪ Use your voice and body language to make your message memorable. Only 7% of your message is perceived by the words you use. The other 93% is from the tone of your voice, the rate of speech and your body language.

↪ Leave participants with handouts, advertising materials and an evaluation form to fill out on the spot. The evaluation is an excellent marketing tool as it provides you with names for your database, testimonials, marketing of your services and referrals for more business (see page 118). Another way to capture names is to hold a drawing. Ask the audience to drop their business cards in a bowl. Then select several people to receive a free book, one-hour complimentary consultation, etc. It's fun. And it generates goodwill for you and builds your database

↪ Finally, don't worry about getting it "right." We've given thousands of talks—every one of them technically flawed. Relax and enjoy yourself, present the "enthusiastic you" and your message will shine through.

RATING SHEET

For Arnold Sanow   Date:_____

Please help us to constantly increase the *VALUE* of our material to you. We appreciate you filling out this form and handing it in at the end of the program.

Name:_____ Title:_____
Company:_____ Phone:_____
Address:_____

What is the **BEST**, usable idea you gained from this program?_____
_____
_____

How do you plan to apply this idea?_____
_____
_____

What do you wish there had been more time for?_____
_____
_____

Your opinion of today's program?_____
_____
_____

May we quote you? Yes _____

WHAT IS YOUR MOST URGENT PROFESSIONAL NEED FROM US?
(Please put an "X" next to all that apply. *We will call you within 3 days.*)

- ☐ Paid Speaking Seminar?
- ☐ Need Educational Materials (Books, Tapes, Videos)?
- ☐ Marketing consultation?
- ☐ Business and Marketing plans?
- ☐ Time management and organization strategies?
- ☐ Business Assessment?
- ☐ Help in getting your products exported overseas?
- ☐ Need a training department? . . . "Lease" one . . . Let us handle all your training needs.

- ☐ Training Program(s) for your company?
- ☐ Presentation Skills Training?
- ☐ Learn to become a paid professional speaker?
- ☐ Marketing Research?
- ☐ Customer service training/consulting?
- ☐ Business Development?
- ☐ Business opportunities?
- ☐ Help in buying/selling a business?
- ☐ Interested in becoming a sales rep for our company?
- ☐ TV/Radio/Print Publicity

Do you belong to a group looking for a Speaker? (The Business Source, Inc., will assist you).

Name of group:_____ Date Speaker needed:_____
Subject:_____
Person in charge:_____ Phone:_____

The Business Source, Inc., 2810 Glade Vale Way, Vienna, VA 22181, (703) 255-3133.

MARKETING BOOT CAMP

Success #**47** Strategy

Heat Up Profits By Igniting Your Creative Fires

Einstein said, "Imagination is more powerful than knowledge." That goes double for advertising and marketing because **innovation and excitement sell!** That means you need to constantly create new and better ways to get your prospects' attention to motivate them to try or buy your product or service. Of course, stretching your creative problem-solving capabilities can help you solve virtually *any* challenge ranging from raising capital to training employees.

The problem is, most people believe they somehow missed the divine "creative gene." Is this you? Well, get over it! Creative thinking is *not* limited to artists and inventors. You're more creative than you may believe. We guarantee it. You just need an open mind and several of the following idea-generating techniques. But beware. Solving marketing challenges or any problem without a *strategy* is like shooting arrows wearing a blindfold. To find the right answers, you have to ask the right questions.

Before you tackle any marketing challenge, you should work hand-in-hand with the *12 Crucial Questions* discussed in Success Strategy #20. This list helps you focus on how your product, service, publication or institution will be meaningfully communicated to consumers' needs, wants, desires and dreams. Your **big ideas** must be *relevant* to this strategy to be successful. Advertising great David Oglivy put it best when he said, "If it doesn't sell, it ain't creative."

Ideas are organic. They're all around us. What we need are techniques to spark our creative fires. Here are several methods that work for us and can work for you:

↪ **Mind Mapping:** Also known as "Clustering," this nonlinear brainstorming process is used to override the "that's a stupid idea" logical left side of your brain with intuitive, right-brained associations emanating from personal experience. On a fresh page, circle a nucleus word or phrase. Write down any connections that relate to the nucleus word as quickly as you can. Circle the new words or phrases and draw lines to related patterns. When you free associate from one idea to another you'll experience a chain reaction that can create an explosion of new thought patterns and ideas. Mind Mapping is a revealing exercise that will help you develop numerous emotion-based ideas. And emotion sells!

↪ **Forced Relationships:** Try and force two seemingly unrelated things or ideas. Pet rocks, Mickey Mouse and clock radios are examples of this technique.

↪ **Make the Familiar Strange and the Strange Familiar:** Remember the '60s Volkswagen ad headline that trumpeted "Lemon"? It was really an ad for quality control that helped sell thousands of bugs. You can also put a spin on clichés, catch phrases and idioms, rework famous quotes, and incorporate irony and metaphor in your creative thinking and writing. Can you take your product or service and shrink it, stretch it, turn it upside down, communicate the opposite?

↪ **Brainstorming:** One of the best ways to arrive at a winning creative solution is to quickly generate a **ton** of ideas by brainstorming with a group or by yourself. One brainstorming path you can take is down the *100 Ideas* road. Coming up with 100 ideas for a product, problem or headline is really not as difficult as it sounds. And while you're producing so many ideas you can tap into your unconscious mind which, when uninterrupted by that ever-present "negative voice of judgment," will yield far more interesting and effective solutions than if you stopped at idea #12. Don't worry. Suspend judgment. Let go. Wild, off-the-wall thoughts are OK too! Finally, after you generate an avalanche of ideas, you must decisively cull them into a single interesting, compelling and effective solution.

⇨ **Idea Bank:** Keep an idea bank or "swipe file" of words, phrases, ads, brochures and sales letters that have gotten **your** attention to help spark new ideas through lateral thinking. Good ideas come at the strangest time—usually when you're not consciously thinking about your challenge (how many "ah-ha's" have you gotten in the shower, for example?). Don't forget to carry a tape recorder (or keep one on your night stand) and index cards to capture your magic moments. Napkins, candy bar wrappers and restaurant placemats work quite well in a pinch!

Never underestimate the powerful potential of your creativity. Always challenge yourself to sidestep shopworn solutions. The sheer joy of the creative process is rewarding in itself. The icing on the cake is that monetary rewards tend to follow those who can solve problems in original ways. We wish you much spontaneous combustion!

Following are samples of **big creative ideas** that have earned $billions for these advertisers. They seem so simple, but you can bet your briefcase that hundreds to thousands of hours and ideas were brainstormed to come up with these profitable gems:

Greyhound: Leave The Driving To Us
Maxwell House: Good To The Last Drop
Federal Express: When It Absolutely, Positively Has To Be There
  Overnight
Clairol: Does She Or Doesn't She?
Kodak Film: A Kodak Moment
Marlboro Country
American Express Travelers Checks: Don't Leave Home Without
  Them

Purdue Chicken: It Takes A Tough Man To Make A Tender
   Chicken
M&M's: Melts In Your Mouth, Not In Your Hands
McDonalds: You Deserve A Break Today
Coke: It's The Real Thing
Prudential: A Piece Of The Rock
Ford: Have You Driven A Ford Lately?
Michelin: Because So Much Is Riding On Your Tires.

Creativity Boosting Resources:
Creativity In Business, by Michael Ray and Rochell Myers
Writing The Natural Way, by Gabrielle Lusser Rico
Whack On The Side Of The Head, by Roger von Oech

There are several exciting computer tools that can help you accelerate the idea-generating process and spark flashes of insight. They can help
you meet challenges ranging from product-naming and headline generation to solving cash flow problems and writing speeches. What this software won't do is solve the problem for you. What it will do is prod and
prompt you into finding relationships and unexpected connections that
may not have surfaced otherwise. One excellent "idea-starter" software
program we recommend is *"Ideafisher"* (for PC or Macintosh). It's a the-
saurus of ideas with over 60,000 words, expressions, people, places and
things cross-referenced in over 700,000 ways. Groupings of common traits
and related concepts can spur new thinking to help you solve marketing
challenges in original ways. Call (301) 946-4284 for details.

SECTION 4

Golden Keys To
Making More Sales

MARKETING BOOT CAMP

Success **#48** Strategy

5 Ways To Get Business Now!

1. **Ask businesses to sponsor you.** The possibilities are endless. Many businesses could promote themselves by having you speak. For example, an electronics store once hired Arnold to provide seminars free of charge to members of the community. The seminar, which was held at the store, brought in potential customers, received media exposure and was perceived as helping the community. In another example, Arnold was hired by a publisher of a magazine to give morning breakfast seminars. The publisher wanted to offer extra value to the customers that advertised in his magazine by giving them additional training on marketing. The publisher received good public relations value, increased the loyalty of his customers and increased his client base. As the speaker, Arnold received a fee and access to many potential clients.

   Both Dan and Arnold are currently being sponsored by various businesses to give their *Marketing Boot Camp* seminars. Various organizations such as banks, advertising agencies, accounting firms and others are using this as an incentive to get new customers and keep their current ones.

2. **Work with and subcontract with others.** If you need business fast, talk to your competitors. In fact, about 20% of our business comes from our competitors. Many times they can't take on a particular project because they're too busy, they don't want to do it, or they're not big enough to handle it. If you can let them know you're available and can be trusted not to steal their clients, then they'll work with you.

3. **Contact your past and current clients.** Call your past and current clients and let them know all of the new or special services you offer. Because they've had a positive experience with your work and you've developed a rapport, they'll be open to additional services. In addition, you should always ask your clients if they know if anyone else who may need your products or services. Never assume that they will just refer you. One of the main reasons for lack of referrals is that many of your current clients may think that you're too busy. From now on, when people ask, "How's business?", don't say that you're really busy. Instead say, "I'm busy, but always looking for more."

4. **Spin off from your past employer.** Past employers know your capabilities. Contact them to work on a part-time or contractual basis. Show them how you can save them money by working on a contractual basis. Point out that they won't have to pay any overhead such as social security taxes, health insurance, and other benefits that can add 33% or more to a salary.

5. **Set up a joint venture with a radio station.** If your expertise is of interest to the general public, you can work an arrangement with a radio station to advertise a seminar or speech (free of charge). You will do the legwork and you both split the fees. For example, if you are an expert on taxes, you may want to have the station sponsor a seminar on the latest tax laws. By doing this you will receive the credibility of the station, free advertising, split fees and future client contacts.

MARKETING BOOT CAMP

Success #**49** Strategy

Lead Generation . . . The Lifeblood Of Your Business

Unfortunately, while diamonds may be forever, many customers are not. The marketplace is constantly shifting. People move away, die, change jobs, create new alliances, etc. Even though you may have a substantial in-house mailing list of prospective customers, to sustain success you need to be vigilant about finding new leads and markets to sell to.

Following are lead-generating resources to consider:

1. **Mailing lists.** The names you acquire through mailing lists are typically rented, not bought, for one-time use. There are 20,000+ mailing lists available and you can select categories ranging from small business owners to credit card customers, buyers of kids' clothing to expectant mothers in their second trimester. You can get geographically targeted lists or isolate people with the same demographics (statistical or behavioral commonalties like old, young, men, women, single, married) or psychographics (people with similar lifestyles or associations). Names typically rent for $25 to $100 per 1,000. Usually, the "hotter" the name, the more it costs. For example, if you're selling a product, newsletter, magazine sub-scription or catalog, name prices are based on the RFM formula— Recency (how long ago they bought), frequency (how often they order) and monetary (how much and what specific products they buy). Your source for mailing lists is the *Direct Mail Lists Rates And Data* published by *Standard Rates and Data Service.*

2. **List brokers.** Brokers will help you locate and evaluate the right lists for your needs. They work like travel agents and receive their commissions from the originating list source. You can find list brokers in the SRDS or in your yellow pages under "Mail Lists." One broker we've had success with is Brant Turner at Dunhill of Washington, (202) 331-7724.

3. **Associations.** Many trade and professional associations make their member names available. You'll want to consider these two resources to reach the lucrative association market:

Encyclopedia of Associations
Gale Research Company
Book Tower
Detroit, MI 48226

National Trade and Professional Associations of America
Columbia Books, Inc.
1212 New York Avenue, NW, Suite 330
Washington, DC 20005
(202) 898-0662

Where Else Can You Find Leads?

➪ Chambers of Commerce rosters
➪ Club and civic organization directories
➪ Newspapers—stories about companies or individuals who are potential prospects
➪ Help wanted ads. The kinds of companies you may be targeting usually list names, addresses and phone numbers. A freelance graphic designer we know responds to ads seeking full-time designers. He sends samples of his work and a letter saying he'd be happy to take on their overflow work. A staggering 50% of these companies hire him for jobs!
➪ "Bingo cards"—sales inquiries generated by trade publication advertising allows prospects to respond to ads by circling numbers on a postage-paid postcard

- ⇨ "Tip in" cards—attached or loose response cards in magazines
- ⇨ Lead-generation ads in newspaper, newsletters, trade publications and radio/television
- ⇨ Bulletin board ads in retail establishments
- ⇨ Electronic bulletin boards via modem (contact CompuServe, Inc., 1-800-848-8199 and Prodigy Information Services, 1-800-766-3449 to get started)
- ⇨ Take-one cards
- ⇨ Store bag stuffers
- ⇨ Established lead or "tipster" groups comprising members from different industries. Or consider starting your own group
- ⇨ Present/past customer referrals
- ⇨ Competitor referrals
- ⇨ Co-op mailings with non-competing companies
- ⇨ Postcard decks
- ⇨ Seminars/workshops
- ⇨ Adult education classes
- ⇨ Speaking/seminar engagements
- ⇨ Networking mixers
- ⇨ Involvement in community/fund raising events
- ⇨ Trade shows
- ⇨ Surveys/questionnaires
- ⇨ Newsletters
- ⇨ Catalogs
- ⇨ Classified/display ads placed by companies you're targeting
- ⇨ Employees
- ⇨ Friends, family

Hint: As your database of customers grows, you'll be able to take advantage of another lucrative income stream. That is, renting your list of names to non-competitors for one-time use. Prices are negotiable but can range from fifty cents to $1.00 per name. There are probably businesses in your own backyard that would love to exchange names or rent your list. Brokers who will help you rent your names can be found in the SRDS book.

MARKETING BOOT CAMP

Success #**50** Strategy

From Inquiry To Client . . .
The Critical Path

When a potential client calls, follow this proven strategy:

1. **Establish Rapport**—Find out who they are, introduce yourself and provide your credibility.
2. **Find Out Needs**—Before selling your services, find out what they are looking for and the outcome(s) they expect to get from using your product or service.
3. **Present Benefits**—Show them how your product or service can help them save, gain or accomplish something.
4. **Resolve Objections**—Review all possible objections and practice the responses.
5. **Trial Close**—Ask them questions such as, "I have an opening for tomorrow, would you like to set up an appointment to start?" or "I could take your credit card number now so we could confirm your space, would you like to do that?"
6. **Set The Meeting**—In most cases the purpose of the call is to arrange a meeting. There's a much better chance you'll close a deal face-to-face than on the phone.

MARKETING BOOT CAMP

Success   #**51**   Strategy

How To Qualify Prospects Instantly

As more and more people respond to your marketing efforts—as they surely will when you begin implementing *The "9/18 Relationship Marketing System"*—you'll find yourself becoming more selective with the quality of prospects. (Doesn't that sound delightful?) That's because you'll be busy handling all of your new-found business!

Caution: There are a myriad of people just itching to waste your time, or addicted to requesting free sales literature. Inevitability, more and more "suspects" will call and "ask for information" with no intention of buying. Occasionally, they'll be your competitors snooping around to see what you're up to. It's your job to sift through the "fools gold" and isolate the bona fide sales prospects from the tire kickers. You can quickly avoid wasting precious time and resources on unqualified prospects by asking several questions to assess their needs and genuine level of interest.

First, tell them you'd be happy to send information but would like to know a little more about them to tailor your mailing to their precise needs. Here are several questions to qualify prospects faster:

1. How did you hear about us?
2. What kind of business are you in? What size?
3. What specific challenges are you facing?
4. What specific product/service are you looking for?
5. What do you know about us?

If after several questions you feel they are not a realistic candidate for your product or service, you may want to get right to the money issue by asking, "What's your budget?"

If you feel you have an opportunity to do business, by all means send along your solution-oriented response package. While you have your prospect on the phone, agree to send the information and immediately set up a telephone or personal appointment to discuss their needs in detail.

If you can't help with your primary product or service perhaps you have a smaller item or service the prospect can take advantage of. One high-end graphic designer we know has set up a "Bare Bones" division to accommodate smaller-budget clients. Another example: If one of our copywriting prospects can't afford our services, we'll recommend this book and other copywriting books to help them write the marketing documents themselves. Always look for a way to provide some level of service. If you've determined they're not total flakes but that you still can't help, you'll want to refer them to someone who can.

MARKETING BOOT CAMP

Success   #**52**   Strategy

Pre-Heat Letters Cure Cold Calls

Cold calls can be hazardous to your mental health . . . and your sales. At best they can be demoralizing and embarrassing. At worst, they can quickly irritate or anger a prospect. The problem with cold calls is that you haven't given someone a *reason* to listen to you or trust you. Now we know that Type Triple-A personalities and masochists have no problems with cold calls, so please be our guests. But if you want to freeze out cold calls, this simple strategy will help you gain a faster foothold with your prospects. It's called a "pre-heat" letter and this is all you have to say:

Dear Mr. Smith:

This letter—and the enclosed brochure (article or whatever)—are by way of introduction to ABC Computers and the services we can provide to help your staff save up to 15 hours a week on laborious, time-consuming data entry duties.

Once you've had a chance to look over the brochure, I'd like to introduce myself over the phone and answer any questions you may have about us.

Sincerely,

Janice Jones

There you have it. A **reason** to call. At the very least, your prospect won't be surprised when you phone. And, from our personal experience, virtually 85% of the people we've called after sending a pre-heat letter remembered us and responded positively to our communication. Oh yes, make sure you call no later than one week after mailing. Of course when you get a referral from someone, you can skip this step and call them immediately. And, please, don't be afraid to make an "information-gathering cold call." If you can build an instant rapport with a prospect, by all means try to set an appointment.

MARKETING BOOT CAMP

Success   #**53**   Strategy

Ring Up More Sales With Your Telephone

You can sell virtually anything over the telephone. For example, following up a mailing with a phone call can increase your response by 10%. You can also boost the response of your print and media ad campaigns using the phone lines. Like all sales, telemarketing is a numbers game and you're going to have to "kiss a lot of frogs to find a prince or princess." You can handle the phones yourself, use in-house telemarketers or hire a telemarketing firm. Consider using telemarketing specialists for lead-generation. By increasing the pool of qualified leads, you'll boost productivity because your sales people will be able to *sell* instead of prospecting. Whether taking calls or making calls, these ideas will help you increase sales and profits.

Winning Telephone Tips

Answer the Phone on the Second or Third Ring.
Answering on the first ring makes you appear too anxious. Answering on the second or third ring shows that your company is on the ball.

Answer With Enthusiasm.
If you're not enthusiastic about your product or service, no one else will be. People are more convinced by your enthusiasm than anything else.

Smile When You Talk.
Smiling subconsciously makes you more upbeat. And people can really tell by your tone if you're smiling or not. To make sure you keep that smile, put a mirror next to your phone. In fact, one telephone company puts a mirror next to each one of its operators' desks.

Never Start Off With an Apology.
You lose control and it dilutes your message.

Sit Up or Stand When Talking.
This opens your diaphragm and allows your voice to unfold naturally.

Introduce Your Company and Then Yourself.
Never ask someone his or her name until you introduce yourself.

Match Their Speaking Speed When Talking.
People communicate best with people who communicate like they do. To persuade and influence, match the communication skills that they think are important.

Limit Your Own Talking.
The more the other person is talking the better chance of closing the sale. In addition, by listening you can find out what he or she really wants and hear any possible objections.

Use Open-Ended Questions.
By asking more than just yes and no questions you can gather more information regarding the caller's needs.

Use the Caller's Name.
As Dale Carnegie says, "The sweetest thing to any person is the sound of their name."

Keep Attention on the Caller.
Eliminate the words "I" "Me" and "Mine" and replace them with "you" and "we."

Keep Your Promises.
If you say you're going to call someone back in an hour . . . do it!

Picture the Person In Your Mind.
Treat each phone call as if it were a face-to-face meeting. By picturing the person in your mind, your thoughts become clearer.

MARKETING BOOT CAMP
Success #**54** Strategy

The Best Times to Call

Accountants	*Daytime except Tax Season*
Bankers	*Before 10:00 after 3:00*
Builders	*Before 9 after 5*
Dentist	*Before 9:30 am*
Management (general)	*After 10:30 am*
Entrepreneurs	*Before 8:30 after 5:00*
Homemakers	*Between 10:00–11:00*
Attorneys	*Between 11:00–2:00*
Minimum wage/part-time	*At home*
Physicians	*Btwn 9:00–11:00; 4:00–5:00*
Publishers	*After 3:00*
Stockbrokers	*Before 10:00–after 3*
Trainers, Instructors	*At home 6:00–7:00*
Home Market	*8:30–11:00 Saturdays*

MARKETING BOOT CAMP

Success **#55** Strategy

The 2-Step, No Stress Telemarketing Success System

Arnold knows first hand how this system works. In fact, this is how he found his financial planner, George Khalsa of Gale Financial Group in Vienna, Virginia. Here's how George landed Arnold's business over the phone lines.

The first call came from his assistant:

> This is Michelle Johnson from the Gale Financial Group. We've just completed our latest client newsletter with articles on beating C.D. rates, reducing insurance costs and personal and business financial planning. If you have an interest in this area we'll send you the newsletter, if that's OK with you.

That sounded good to Arnold, who said, "Send it." Now here's the significant point: she confirmed Arnold's address, said she would mail the newsletter, told Arnold that the author would get back to him some time in the future, and got off the phone. No pressure. The whole conversation took a couple of minutes.

A week or so later the author called.

> Hello, this is George Khalsa from the Gale Financial Group. A week ago you spoke with my assistant Michelle; we're the people who sent you the newsletter, the Khalsa report. During the last 12 years I've worked with a lot of people and businesses with regard to their financial planning. I'm suggesting we meet for 20 minutes to see if there is anything we can do that you feel is worth exploring further. I'm wondering if, in the next few weeks, you can fit me into your schedule for 20 minutes.

Clearly this is a low-pressure, low-stress strategy you can use for your clients and prospects. But according to George Khalsa, the major benefit of this approach is that there is no stress to the caller because he or she is not getting killed with rejection. One out of three prospects says "yes" to the literature and one out of those three agrees to an appointment.

Where telemarketing is appropriate for your business, this system will work for you. Substitute your name, product or service in George's script and put together a nice one-page information sheet on your business. Remember not to make it too specific or too much of a hard sales pitch. Now dial "R" for relationship and ring up those sales!

Dialing for Dollars . . .
8 Rules for Getting Through

⇨ Ask for help from the switchboard operator.

⇨ Start from the top down if you don't know the decision maker.

⇨ Give as little information as possible about why you are calling.

⇨ Ask for "Jim Jones"—not "*Mr.* Smith."

⇨ Answer a question with a question—"Joe Jones from XYZ Company. Can you connect me please?"

⇨ Use a firm businesslike tone—assertive but friendly. Have a sense of urgency.

⇨ When asked "What is this in reference to?" have a prepared vague statement.

⇨ Never leave your telephone number.

MARKETING BOOT CAMP

Success **#56** Strategy

Make Your Voice Mail Sell

How many times do you hear this kind of message on a business' voice mail or answering machine: *"Hello, thank you for calling the International Marketing Institute. We're unavailable to take your call right now. Please leave you name and number after the tone and we'll get right back to you."* BEEP.

If you don't already have a benefit-oriented message on your voice mail, you're throwing away yet another chance to sell. Here's how the message above would sound using an extended version of the *"16-Second Sizzler"* technique.

> *Welcome to the voice mail of the International Marketing Institute. This is Dan McComas speaking. If you're looking for ways to make more money with your marketing, we can help you in three ways:*
>
> > *One: By creating your cash-generating ads, flyers, sales letters, brochures and publicity.*
> > *Two: Through our highly-acclaimed Marketing Boot Camp seminars and keynote speeches.*
> > *And Three: By ordering the money-making books and tapes in our Unfair Advantage Marketing Success Guide—It's free for the asking!*
>
> *Please leave your name, number and the ways we can help you succeed this year.*

Now, when a prospect calls, they'll understand and remember the specific products and services you provide. And isn't that what you want?

MARKETING BOOT CAMP
Success #**57** Strategy

5 Ways To Overcome Call Reluctance

Do you ever go through those times when you get so many rejections you never want to see a phone again? To be successful in marketing, all of us have to use the phone lines. To deal with "caller reluctance," follow these five guidelines:

1. **Saturate Yourself with Positive Upbeat Feelings**—Use positive affirmations and keep saying to yourself over and over, "I'm energetic, enthusiastic, and effective. I'm prepared, poised and persuasive." You are what your thoughts are. Positive mental conditioning helps you to trigger a favorable response.

2. **Prepare Yourself Technically**—Keep practicing your lines. Like an actor on Broadway you need to constantly study and improve. Be prepared to answer all responses, reactions and questions you might generate. Knowing your products or services inside out gives you the competitive edge and confidence you'll need to succeed.

3. **Focus on the Rewards of Success, Not the Penalty of Failure**—Look at every call as a potential opportunity that can change your entire week, month or even year. Picture how you will feel after a big sale. You will always be rewarded in direct proportion to your efforts.

4. **Remember People Are Nice**—Most people you call will be pleasant. They are just like you. If you think the potential buyer is tough it will be reflected in your attitude . . . and you will set your own scenario for failure.

5. **Most People May Not Show They Are Nice Right Away**—It's not that people are naturally testy, but they may have had a bad experience in the past or are nervous, tense or insecure.

Resource: *Earning What You're Worth? The Psychology of Sales Call Reluctance,* by George W. Dudley and Shannon L. Goodson (Behavioral Sciences Research Press, Inc.)

MARKETING BOOT CAMP

Success **#58** Strategy

Listen, Learn And Earn More

Many people assume that to be good in sales you need to talk . . . talk . . . talk. This couldn't be further from the truth. In fact, the best sales people are those who listen. By listening you not only become more popular but you also learn and earn more. To become an active listener follow these rules:

- ➪ Limit your own talking.
- ➪ Concentrate on the person who is talking.
- ➪ Don't interrupt.
- ➪ Paraphrase what has been said.
- ➪ Talk in a conducive setting.
- ➪ See things from the other person's viewpoint.
- ➪ Notice nonverbal communication.
- ➪ Don't prejudge.
- ➪ Don't just think of what you're going to say next.

HOW GOOD A LISTENER ARE YOU?

Right now you might be thinking, "Who needs all this talk about listening? I'm a good listener!" Are you, really? Let us suggest that you first take the following test yourself; then ask two of the people with whom you communicate most frequently to rate you on the same statements.

Listening Test

(Number a sheet of paper from 1 to 20, then rate yourself on a scale of 1 [low rating] to 5 [high rating] on each of the following statements. Ask two friends to rate you on the same scale and compare your findings.)

1. I always attempt to give every person I talk with equal time to talk.
2. I really enjoy hearing what other people have to say.
3. I never have difficulty waiting until someone finishes talking so that I can have my say.

4. I listen even when I do not particularly like the person talking.
5. The sex and age of a person makes no difference in how well I listen.
6. I assume every person has something worthwhile to say and listen intently to friends, acquaintances and strangers alike.
7. I put away what I am doing while someone is talking.
8. I always look directly at the person who is talking and give that person my full attention, no matter what is on my mind.
9. I encourage others to talk by giving them verbal feedback and asking questions.
10. I encourage other people to talk by my non-verbal messages, such as gestures, facial expressions and posture.
11. I ask for clarification of words and ideas I do not understand.
12. I am sensitive to the tone of the speaker's voice, expressions and gestures that convey meaning.
13. I never interrupt a person who is talking.
14. I withhold all judgements and opinions about what a person is saying until I have heard it all.
15. I listen past the words to the feelings and meanings the person is expressing, and test to see if I am understanding correctly.
16. I make mental outlines of the main points of what a person is saying.
17. I look mainly for points on which we can agree, not mainly for points on which we disagree.
18. I respect every person's right to his or her opinions, even if I disagree with them.
19. I view every dispute or conflict as an opportunity to understand the person better.
20. I recognize that listening is a skill and I concentrate on trying to develop that skill in my daily life.

Scoring: Add up the total point value of your ratings and score them as follows: 90–100, You're all ears; 80–89, You're a pretty good listener; 70–79, You're missing a lot; and 69 and under, it might be a good idea to have your ears checked.

The fact is that all of us can improve our skills at listening. It is equally true that by improving our skills at listening, we can improve our skills as communicators.

Reprinted with permission of Nido Qubein, "Communicate Like a Pro," Berkley Publishing.

MARKETING BOOT CAMP

Success #**59** Strategy

It's Not *What* You Say, But *How* You Say It

Only 7% of the messages people perceive are through the words you use. Another 38% come through the tone of your voice and 55% are communicated through your body language. To enhance your presentation skills and how you are perceived by others, follow these golden rules:

Use Good Eye Contact
In other words, focus on the person you're talking to. You don't want to stare, but you do want to keep your eyes on them and occasionally look away. If you don't look at them, likability and trust are lost.

Smile
People would much rather deal with someone who is upbeat and happy than someone who is dour. As Walt Disney said, "You get paid for smiling."

Be Enthusiastic
People are more convinced by your enthusiasm than anything else. Remember, if you're not enthusiastic about your product or service, will anyone else be?

Use Humor
Humor makes you more likable. Also people will remember what you're saying.

Beware of Distractions
Certain things like ring twisting, tapping your pencil, and interrupting conversations will take the focus away from you and your message. For example, Arnold was talking to a potential client and noticed his prospect wasn't listening. Arnold asked him if there was a reason and the man said he was wondering what was attached to Arnold's shirt sleeve. It was the laundry ticket from the dry cleaner!

Use Stories and Anecdotes
Create mental pictures. The more you can create a picture in someone's mind, the easier it is to persuade him or her to your way of thinking.

Prepare What You Want To Say In Advance
As Abraham Lincoln said, "I can give a rambling two-hour speech right now, but if you want a concise 20-minute speech, I'll need three weeks to prepare." Whether you're talking to a large group or making a sales presentation, planning and preparation will help you become more persuasive and get what you want!

MARKETING BOOT CAMP

Success #**60** Strategy

Overcoming Objections To Your Product Or Service

How you handle objections brought up by potential customers can either make or break sales. You need to be adept not only at handling obstacles and objections, but also at countering these objections in a tactful manner. Our ultimate goal in handling these objections skillfully is to close more sales. To be successful at handling objections you need to anticipate what they are and how to react to them. Objections should be something you look forward to. By giving you objections, the potential customer shows he or she is alert and interested in your presentation. In fact, every objection is an opportunity to develop the sale further.

Most people average between six to eight objections before they make the sale. The best way to handle any objection is to know as much as possible about your product or service, your company, your markets, your competition, your sales presentation and yourself. To make sure you effectively handle objections follow these eight strategies:

1. **Display a Positive Attitude Toward the Objection and the Prospect.** Once you start showing annoyance in your voice or posture, the odds of getting the customer to agree or buy become diminished.
2. **Always Listen Carefully to the Complete Objection.** By listening to the entire objection you can usually determine the *real* problem.

3. **Know When to Answer the Objection.** The best time to answer an objection is immediately after it's raised. If you wait too long, prospects will feel that you lack knowledge, fear something or you don't believe in the product or service. In addition their trust in you becomes eroded.

4. **Restate the Objection.** This shows you are concerned and allows you the opportunity to make sure the perceived objection is correct.

5. **Give Brief Answers.** Answer objections in a straightforward, clear, sincere and genuine manner. If you avoid the objection or dance around it the prospect will lack trust in you and your product or service.

6. **Tailor the Reply of the Objection to the Prospect.** Don't have standard answers for everyone. Each prospect is different. Tailor your reply to specifically match the prospect's buying motives.

7. **Observe How Customers Express Objections.** Keep an eye on customers' body language. If they have an objection and they're smiling, it's usually a sign that the objection is not too important. On the other hand, if they're leaning forward in their chair, they start crossing their arms and they cross their legs in the opposite direction from you, then you better take the objection more seriously.

8. **Recognize Times When the Objection is Final.** One of the most important factors for your future success is goodwill. By keeping on friendly terms with the prospect, your name will have a positive connotation. Many times you will receive referrals and be kept in mind for possible work in the future.

MARKETING BOOT CAMP

Success **#61** Strategy

Typical Objections . . . What To Say

Objection: *"Your price is too high."*

To get to the core of this objection, answer it with a question like, "Why do you feel the price is too high?" Focus on value, not price. For example, one professional speaker we know gets $15,000 a speech. This seems like a very high price but the person is well known and the sponsoring organization will get a sellout crowd. In addition, the sponsor can charge a higher attendance fee. Also, be sure your prospect is comparing apples to apples. If not, point out the features, benefits and other advantages your product or service provides that make it worth the price. You can also break down the price into bite-size chunks to make it easier to swallow. And don't forget to tout the ultimate benefit. That is, the incredible service *you* will offer!

Objection: *"We've had problems with your company or product/service before."*

Apologize that something like this has happened. Get all the facts and circumstances and determine what can be or has been done to correct the problem. Then take action by explaining the specific steps you will take to make sure something like this will not happen again.

Objection: *The prospect may not feel a need for your product or service.*

Your task is to *create* a compelling want by triggering on prospects' rational and/or emotional motivations. Some methods to create this want include:

1. Show that your new product has extra features/benefits that outweigh the potential cost.
2. Demonstrate how they can actually save money by getting the service now.
3. Indicate the risks involved by not buying your product or service now.
4. Show how the product or service will help them save, gain or accomplish something.

Objection: *To the service or product offered.*

Some ways to handle this objection include:

1. Show them proof-positive written testimonials.
2. Give a list of references.
3. Give a guarantee.
4. Show them positive magazine/newspaper articles about the product or service.

Objection: *To a characteristic or trait of the product or service.*

Objections may be based on a small feature that disturbs the prospect. The strategy here is to show why that certain characteristic is beneficial or important. For example, if someone is buying a car and you have exactly what they like, but it's in yellow and they're not crazy about that color, stress statistical evidence that yellow cars get into fewer accidents.

MARKETING BOOT CAMP

Success #**62** Strategy

Key Closing Strategies
To Make The Sale Happen

Everything you do is really leading up to your ultimate goal . . . closing sales! Without this important element your business won't last long. Many people ask, "When is the best time to close the sale?" The answer is . . . *as soon as you can!* The way you close a sale depends on the service or product you're selling and even more importantly the customer you're dealing with. Some of the proven methods for closing sales include:

Summarize
For potential clients who like to think things through before making a decision, this is a very successful technique. You can reassure them by reiterating the features and benefits and by making sure there were no points that were overlooked.

Advantages and Disadvantages
At the end of your presentation list the pros and cons.

Close on an Objection
In this method, the salesperson must determine what the real objection is. If the objection is a block to the sale, you must answer it directly and assume the close.

Offering a Premium
The "something for nothing" technique. This method focuses on offering the prospect a gift or reward for buying now.

Limited Offer

The quickest way to create a desire for ownership in many people is to tell them they cannot have what they have expressed interest in. For example, if you give training seminars and you only have one day open in the next three months, you want to let prospective attendees know that they need to sign up immediately or the opportunity may be lost.

The Low-key Approach

People don't like to be pressured. They like to buy but they don't like to be sold. By planning your presentation carefully and by understanding the wants and needs of the potential client, you'll make more than your share of sales. For example, you may want to say, "Thank you for your time, the next step is for us to get together to see if this program is right for you." By being sincere, you'll put the potential client into a relaxed mood and increase his or her willingness to work with you.

Close on a Minor Point

This technique is used with prospects who cannot make a major buying decision. The salesperson stresses minor decisions of when to buy rather than whether, and which to buy rather than if. By closing on small points the major buy becomes obvious.

Guarantee It

Make it a "nothing to lose" proposition.

Suggest Ownership

This technique uses words such as "when," "will" and "would" instead of "if" throughout the presentation or demonstration. By implying ownership and helping prospects imagine the benefits they'll get, you will align them to your way of thinking.

Ask for the Order Directly

This closing technique works well with professional buyers and purchasing managers. Dan's banker did an excellent job of this. While talking on the phone she noted that Dan had his business account with her bank, but not his personal checking account. She said, "Dan, we would love to have your personal checking business; what can we do to make that happen?" After Dan presented a mild "convenience factor" objection, she immediately agreed to waive one of the bank's fees to make it easy for Dan to become a customer. He did. But only because she "asked for the order" and made it easier to buy.

Why Sales Don't Go Through—
12 Common Mistakes

- ➪ Not asking questions
- ➪ Forgetting to talk solutions
- ➪ Jumping ahead of what the prospect is saying
- ➪ Showing no empathy or sympathy
- ➪ Rushing the prospect
- ➪ Being inconsistent
- ➪ Not being an attentive listener
- ➪ Interrupting the prospect
- ➪ Approaching a prospect who is not financially qualified
- ➪ Allowing office distractions (i.e., taking phone calls while talking to prospect)
- ➪ Not handling objections effectively
- ➪ Not asking for the order!

MARKETING BOOT CAMP

Success #**63** Strategy

6 Pricing Mistakes To Avoid

Setting Your Price Too Low

A client of ours is a beginning consultant. One of her strategies to get clients was to keep her fees low. But business was still slow. When we asked potential clients why they didn't select her, many responded, "If she's as good as she claims why is her price is so low?" Many times people equate price with quality. Look at your particular industry to see what the going rates are. You may be amazed at what the market will bear.

Too High of a Price

Although a low price can be a problem, a high price can have the same effect. Again, look at the average rate or fees for your industry. If people object to your price ask these questions:

Aside from price, what do you think?

What would you be willing to pay?

Do you feel this is the service you need or want?

Do you intend to seek out the lowest priced service?

Do you realize that your investment breaks down to only $20.00 per person?

Raising Prices

People become used to prices. When a price or fee is raised many times there is a reluctance to buy that product or service. To overcome this problem, offer a premium to compensate for the higher price. For example, an accountant may want to offer extra time or give clients a software program. If you're selling a product you may want to extend the guarantee or give customers a bonus product when they buy.

Giving Away Free Services

If you keep giving away your services people won't value you or your service. To stop this, the next time someone starts asking you for advice, politely hand them your card and say, "Let me give you my card so we can set up an appointment." Appointment connotes a fee.

Not Stressing Value

Don't push price, focus on the value they will get from using your product or service. For example, if the set fee for the project you are offering is $30,000, focus on how that investment will make them $100,000.

Not Knowing Competitors' Prices and
What They Give for That Price

If you're not aware of your competitors' products, services and prices, then you can't show prospects where you have the advantages. Or, a potential client may say, "Your competitor does this" and if you don't know the competitor's business, you can't come back with a persuasive response. But, if you do know the competitor, you can say, "They have a good company, but we provide these three services above and beyond theirs." Also, remember never to malign a competitor. It will cost you business.

MARKETING BOOT CAMP

Success #**64** Strategy

Strategic Alliances . . . Piggybacking For New Profit Centers

"Companies should expand beyond their existing resources through licensing arrangements, strategic alliances, and supplier relationships."— BUSINESS WEEK

Strategic alliances or joint ventures are the joining of two or more companies to exchange resources, share risks or divide rewards from a mutual enterprise. According to Curtis E. Sahakian in *"Corporate Partnering"* (1-800-948-1700), it's an effective method for acquiring new customers, capital and innovative new products and to adapt to fast-changing markets and technologies. Partnering also allows you to exploit your strengths and shore up your weaknesses. Here are two examples from Sahakian.

NEC Rockets Past Its Competitors
In the 1980s, NEC used more than 100 joint ventures to gain a leading position in three critical high-tech markets: computers, semiconductors and telecommunications. During a period of eight years NEC grew more than five-fold, from $4 billion in sales to more than $20 billion. It shot past its competitors and emerged as one of the leading international companies with in-depth competence in all three key markets. NEC did this while spending a far smaller portion of its revenues on research and development than its competitors.

Beverage Start-Up Gets A Big Boost From Anheuser-Busch
Soho Natural Soda, a start-up producer of natural carbonated beverages, was being operated out of a Brooklyn, NY, kitchen. It didn't have the money to build, rent or operate any bottling facilities. Soho persuaded a regional beer company to use its excess capacity to bottle the beverages and then convinced brewer Anheuser-Busch to distribute the product. In 11 years, it grew from a kitchen table company to $11 million in sales. And Soho did all this with little overhead or cost.

More Mutual Money-making Alliances

⇨ Fast food establishments jointly market with toy companies and entertainment firms to build excitement for their pizzas and burgers. If you're a parent with young children, you (and your waistline) already know how effective these alliances can be in securing your patronage.

⇨ A carpet retailer could join forces with a carpet cleaning company, a drapery company and an interior designer to market their products and services as a convenient shopping "package."

⇨ An optometrist could provide eye examinations in an eyewear retail establishment to offer one-stop shopping for customers.

⇨ A personal "partnering" example is this book you're now reading. Because we teamed up, we were able to write and publish it faster than we could have alone. We've also joined forces as *Marketing Boot Camp* seminar leaders.

Think hard for a moment. What company and supplier relationships or licensing agreements can you tap into right now to generate new profit centers?

MARKETING BOOT CAMP

Success #**65** Strategy

Reactivate Old Leads And Dormant Accounts

If you've been in business for over a year, you're probably sitting on a dormant goldmine. Many of the prospects and customers you've communicated with or served in the past are waiting to hear from you again. Chances are you haven't connected with them often enough, or you haven't presented compelling benefits and offers.

Virtually every business loses accounts or customers through misunderstandings or because a supplier goofed. Sound familiar? In some instances, you may lose a person or company's business and never know why because you failed to ask.

You'll find that a reactivation campaign is less expensive than soliciting new buyers. And you'll probably be pleasantly surprised at how many of these "lost" customers will buy from you again if you'll only contact them. So, blow the dust off those golden names in your database right now and make them an offer they can't refuse! Success Strategy #19 will fuel your thinking.

MARKETING BOOT CAMP

Success   #**66**   Strategy

How To Revitalize A Tired Product Or Service

If your business is slowing down or in decline, put some life into it by asking yourself, your staff and your customers these questions:

Can the product be put to other uses? Other uses if modified? . . . Remember baking soda? When its initial demand diminished, it was repositioned as an effective product for eliminating refrigerator odors.

Can it be adapted? What else is like this? What other ideas does this suggest? What could we copy?

Can it be modified? Given a new twist? Changed in color, meaning, motion, sound, odor, form, shape? Any other changes possible?

Can it be magnified? What to add? More time? Greater frequency? Stronger? Higher? Longer? Shorter? Any other possible changes?

What can we substitute? What else instead? Other ingredients? Other Process? Other power?

Rearrange? Interchange components? Other patterns? Other layouts? Transpose cause and effect? Change the pace? Change the schedule?

Reverse it? Transpose positive and negative? Turn it backward? Upside down? Reverse roles?

Combine it? How about a blend? An assortment? An ensemble? Combine units? Purposes?

MARKETING BOOT CAMP

Success #**67** Strategy

Trade Shows . . .
Where Prospects Come To *You!*

Wouldn't it be nice to have hundreds or even thousands of potential customers visit you? One of today's best strategies for making your selling easier, less costly and more profitable is to become an exhibitor at a trade show.

There are thousands of trade shows throughout the USA and overseas every year offering opportunities for sellers and buyers to meet face to face, share products or services with pre-selected audiences with specific interests, do comparative shopping to shorten the buying process, maintain a positive image, continue contact with potential customers and qualified buyers, introduce a new product or service, investigate the competition and conduct market research. One of the best ways to find out about where and when Trade Shows are taking place is through *"Gayles Encyclopedia of Associations."* This resource can be found at almost any public library. Other references include: *Tradeshow Week Magazine,* (213) 826-5696; *Tradeshow Week Data Book,* (617) 964-3030; and *Trade Show Bureau,* (303) 860-7626.

To ensure your success at trade shows, follow these guidelines:

1. Set your goals. In determining what shows to get into you need to know who are the types of people you need to meet and what shows they attend.
2. Be proactive. Don't just sit in your booth; interact with people who pass. You will miss a lot opportunities if you wait for people to stop and ask questions.
3. Give immediate attention to people entering your booth. Trade show attendees hate to wait. Make sure you have at least two people at the booth so you can engage people walking by and interact with browsers.

4. Develop a 60-second presentation—You need to have a quick and to-the-point presentation describing your product/service and the benefits you offer. First find out if they're qualified, then go into your presentation.

5. Stress benefits—Product and service benefits should be communicated immediately in your oral presentation and visually through your booth displays. Draw them to your booth by having an interesting sign, display, photo, video or even music.

6. Qualify your prospects:
   ⇨ Can they afford your product/service?
   ⇨ Can the prospect influence the purchase?
   ⇨ Is there a need for your product/service?
   ⇨ Determine the visitor's place in the buying cycle.
   ⇨ Establish date of application or purchase.
   ⇨ Be aware of body language.

7. Probe and interview for buying cues. Listen for cues such as "when" can I order this or "can" I get it in red.

8. Record information about the prospect and get a business card. Write any additional information about the prospect on the business card.

9. Stress "What's in it for them." Present the benefits and features. Show them what they can save, gain or accomplish by purchasing your product or service.

10. Offer proof—show credibility. Have testimonials, articles, guarantees, pictures of people using your product or service, television interviews and others.

11. Establish a closing agreement or arrange appointments at the show. Attendees at shows are looking at a lot of different exhibits. Give them an appointment card stating that you will call at a certain time in the future.

12. Follow-up after the show. This is the biggest mistake many exhibitors make. They fail to follow up. If you don't do this the time and expense of the trade show will be a disappointment.

MARKETING BOOT CAMP

Success **#68** Strategy

Back End Sales . . .
Marketing With An Afterlife

"A wise man (or woman) will make more opportunities than he or she finds." — SIR FRANCIS BACON

Reselling customers, members, subscribers and donors is the fastest, easiest and least costly way to increase profitability. Yet every day, well-intentioned marketers leave millions of dollars on the table because they fail to resell or upgrade their buyers. Why is this? Is it the thrill of the new business chase that diverts their attention? Is it simply human nature to become complacent after a victory? A recent survey revealed that during a one-year period, sales representatives participating in the study called on only 61% of their customers while ignoring the other 39%. What's more you probably have a 1-in-15 chance of making a new sale and a 1-to-2 chance of getting a current customer to buy again.

Your profit possibilities are endless when you regularly "resell" your customers.

Once people purchase your product or service and are pleased, they'll buy again. Better still, in most cases they'll buy even more from you. Never forget this: *Your customers are your most important business asset.* Here are 15 opportunities to help them buy again and again!

1. Expand existing services.
2. Introduce new product lines.
3. Extend a service contract.
4. Create a frequent buyer or "VIP" customer club.
5. Hold private sales for preferred customers.
6. Offer package pricing or volume discounts.
7. Offer rebate/special price certificate stuffers in your fulfillment packages or invoice mailings.
8. Relax payment terms to make it easier to buy more.
9. Offer new services to your customers via co-op mailings with non-competitive companies and reap a percentage of the profits.
10. Offer a "today only" special price on a different product after someone has made the intended purchase.
11. Give away gift certificates.
12. Hold a drawing; tell your customers they've won a prize they must pick up at your store. When they arrive, offer them additional products at special discounts.
13. Issue life-time discount cards.
14. Announce overstock promotions.
15. Hold two-for-one sales.

MARKETING BOOT CAMP

Success   #**69**   Strategy

5 Tips For Doing Business With The Federal Government

Mike Stoll, President of Street Smart Seminars, 1-800-736-0031, has been selling consulting and training services to the federal government for years. He has been ignored, shut out and stiffed. On the other hand, he has also been paid early and given preferential treatment. "It's all in understanding how the procurement system works in the government," he says. Here, Mike offers five tips that have helped him and his clients gain lucrative contracts.

1. **Be humble.** When first approaching an agency your attitude should be one of, "I need your help." Even if you think you know what to do and how to do it, seek their advice. You will find out who the decision makers are with greater ease. Be a humble citizen in need of guidance. Eventually they will get to know and befriend you, resulting in your getting the inside knowledge required to close a sale.

2. **Be a helper.** After you get to know the right people your approach should be to help them. Offer to lighten their burden by suggesting design specifications or service requirements that will benefit the government (it's to your benefit if these suggestions match your product or service's uniqueness).

   Caution: This is not a good procurement policy (from the government's point of view) but the facts are that some offices just don't have the people power or the technical experience to write sound bid requirements. Your help here can make you a very favorable vendor during the purchasing process.

3. **Know your customer.** Every agency works a little differently, so it is imperative that you find out who can make or break your success. There are two basic players that will be making buying decisions:

   ➪ The procurement office. People here are trained in contract negotiating, they know the rules of the federal acquisition process and are knowledgeable in budget matters.

   ➪ The end user. These are the people who will have to live with the outcome of a purchasing decision and the people you will have to live with. End users are often very knowledgeable about the products and services they need.

   Some agencies rely solely on the procurement office to make acquisition and purchase decisions, leaving the end user out of the process except for the initial request and some consultation. Other agencies allow the end user to greatly influence the purchasing decision because of their expertise and knowledge of what works best for them. You must play both sides of the street and find the real decision makers. Ask procurement for the end user names and phone numbers and ask end users for procurement names and phone numbers.

4. **Know the rules of the game.** If you're going to sell to the federal government you must learn every method used to acquire goods and services. It's a very complicated system that takes years to learn. Even then the rules are constantly changing. But it is well worth the effort. To help you get started here are some phone numbers that will point you in the right direction:

   ➪ General Services Administration, Business Service Center—(202) 708-5804. The people at this center are here to help all businesses learn the process of federal procurement. They offer counseling and lots of free information on the system.

   ➪ Small Business Administration—1-800-827-5722. Here you can get help from business assistance and counseling, Section 8A minority set asides and the small business advocates that each government agency is required to make available.

↪ Government Printing Office—(202) 783-3238. GPO is where you can purchase essential books and subscriptions such as the Federal Acquisition Regulations (FAR) and the Commerce Business Daily (CBD). The FAR contains the rules of procurement for the government and the CBD is a daily subscription where the government advertises its needs for goods and services.

5. **Getting Paid.** The one area that gets a poor reputation in the government is getting your money. Being successful here is in fact the same as winning business. You must know and play by the rules. One mistake that vendors make is trying to collect from the wrong people. Here are some helpful facts:

↪ Always have a proper purchase order number on your invoice.

↪ Mail your invoice to the address indicated on the purchase order. This is a very common mistake.

↪ When problems occur start by calling the finance office noted on the purchase order, not your customer or the procurement office unless you are advised.

↪ Keep detailed records and get everything in writing. If there is not a written order the government does not have to pay.

The government will always pay you and even pay your late fees if your paperwork is in order. As Mike Stoll says, "I have actually walked out of the Pentagon with cash in my hand because my records were more accurate than theirs, but I've also been unable to prove that services were delivered, resulting in my not being paid." The moral: play By the rules and the rewards will come.

MARKETING BOOT CAMP

Success #**70** Strategy

Writing Winning
Government Proposals

According to Jayme Sokolow, President of The Development Source, every year our local, state and federal governments award over $200 billion in contracts for goods and services ranging from nursing uniforms to computer training. Over half goes to small business.

Although your business probably cannot build the Navy's next nuclear submarine, you win contracts by convincing government agencies you are the best qualified to assist them. Before you write a proposal, however, you should ask yourself three simple questions:

Does the government need my product or service?
Will it be profitable for me?
Am I willing to invest the time and effort to develop a competitive proposal?
If you can answer yes to these three questions, you are ready to proceed.

Step 1: Research your opportunities.
Establish your own information system by contacting the nearest regional Small Business Administration office for assistance. You should also contact procurement officers in government agencies about guidelines, possible competitors and procurement forecasts for the fiscal year. Identify government agencies announcing RFPs (Request for Proposals) for your product or service. And don't neglect local and state governments. They regularly announce contract opportunities and even sponsor small business seminars to help you bid.

Step 2: Prepare a Proposal Strategy.
Think of your proposal as a good sales presentation that demonstrates how you can help a government agency solve its problem. Show that you are technically and professionally competent, dependable, committed to completing the job, capable of understanding and addressing the contract requirements, and cost efficient.

To make your strongest case, carefully study the evaluation factors described in the RFP. They indicate what topics you must address and how much they will be weighed.

Step 3: Prepare your proposal.
Remember the four "c's"—your proposal should be complete, clear, concise and convincing. Proposal formats vary from agency to agency, but all of them contain these elements:

- ⇨ Introduction. Who are you? Do you understand the RFP requirements and have a sound strategy for supplying a product or service?
- ⇨ Discussion of Requirements. What is the problem? How will you solve it? What are the benefits of your plan?
- ⇨ Proposed Program. What is your program and schedule? Where and how will it take place? Why is it the best and most efficient strategy?
- ⇨ Experience and Qualifications. What past experiences and skills qualify you to fulfill this contract?
- ⇨ Evaluation. How will you monitor and measure the success of your project?
- ⇨ Budget. How much will your project cost? How are your costs justified in relationship to your tasks?
- ⇨ Schedule. What is your basic workplan and timeline?
- ⇨ Appendices. What evidence and exhibits will strengthen your argument?

If you need assistance, don't be afraid to contact business colleagues or hire a consultant.

Step 4: Revise and Polish.
After finishing the first draft, revise with these rules in mind: be specific; use action verbs and active voice; avoid sexist language, hyperbole, spelling and grammatical errors; and convey a tone of quiet confidence. Have others review your proposal and provide candid comments. You should spend as much time revising as it took to complete the first draft.

Step 5: Learn from your experiences.
If your proposal is funded by a government agency, congratulations! But if your business does not win the contract, formally request copies of any written evaluations and attend the competition's debriefing session. Many highly successful bidders begin with rejections. Don't be discouraged— be persistent and optimistic. Learn from your experience and try again.

An excellent resource for helping you write your proposal is Jayme Sokolow. He can be contacted at the Development Source, 4312 Garrett Park Road, Wheaton, Maryland 20906, (301) 933-3989.

MARKETING BOOT CAMP

Success   #**71**   Strategy

Audio And Video "Brochures" Cut Through The Clutter

Sending an audio tape or "audio brochure" to promote yourself and your services is a unique way to connect with busy, hard-to-reach prospects. Todd Taskey, a Financial Planner with Solutions Planning Group, Inc., uses audio tapes as a sound strategy for acquiring clients. On the tape, Todd gives several ideas and techniques for enhancing your personal wealth and then offers a brief explanation of his services. A narrator interviews him in a question and answer format that lasts about 15 minutes.

He sends out tapes to a mailing list of potential clients with similar incomes. As Todd says, "The people I deal with are very busy and since many people are getting bombarded with direct mail, I decided to try this unique approach. I've found that by giving them a tape that they can listen to during their down time or while in the car, I can get my message across." Todd is convinced that the audio tape strategy generates new clients faster than other marketing techniques he's tried.

To get a sample tape ($6.00) and information on vendors to help put your audio brochure together, contact Todd Taskey at Solutions Planning Group, Inc., 3 Metro Center, #900, Bethesda, Maryland 20814, (301) 951-5544.

Video Brochures—There's no question Americans are reading less. The U.S. has two full generations who now rely on television as their primary source of information. According to nationally-acclaimed producer Bill Myers, video brochures and video catalogs are ideal ways to showcase products, services or procedures that may be difficult to explain in printed documents. Additionally, videos can be effective training and sales prospecting tools. And they don't have to cost an arm and a leg. Many videos can be produced for hundreds instead of thousands of dollars. Call (301) 946-4284 regarding low-cost video production.

MARKETING BOOT CAMP

Success #*72* Strategy

Boost Sales 85% With A
Credit Card Merchant Account

If you don't already accept credit card payments you're losing money. We sell more books, seminars and copywriting services because we take VISA, MasterCard and American Express. Credit cards make it easy for people to buy and keep records. Additionally, your company appears more credible to the general public. Here are several steps you can take for acquiring merchant status.

If you're a retailer with a store or shop, or a dentist, doctor, etc., you should have no problem becoming a merchant through your bank.

If, however, you are a start-up or home-based business, or sell via phone and mail, 99% of the time your merchant appeal will fall on deaf ears at a bank. That's because some $250 billion has been lost through mail order fraud and canceled purchases. Credit card suppliers just don't want to get burned anymore.

If you've run into brick walls at banks, here are two contacts that will work with you to establish a merchant account. Both organizations can also help you set up a program to take check payments by phone:

First Choice Merchant Systems
1-800-944-7164

National Association of Credit
Card Merchants
(407) 737-7500

And if you need help taking calls and processing orders, there are many 800-number services that will take your orders 24 hours a day, 365 days a year. Two that we can recommend to you are:

Perfect Response Company
1-800-889-1201

Mountain West Communications
1-800-642-9378

SECTION 5

Keeping Customers Coming Back

MARKETING BOOT CAMP

Success **#73** Strategy

Be Relentlessly Customer-Driven To Succeed In The '90s And Beyond

According to Tom Peters, "If you're customer-oriented, you're ahead of 98% of the other businesses because they're not." *Time Magazine* states, "The key to business success for the '90s and beyond will directly correlate to how well you treat your customers." In fact, a survey by the United States Chamber of Commerce proves the importance of customer service. The survey asked people why they don't continue to patronize certain businesses. The answers to why people leave are as follows:

3% move away
5% develop other friendships
9% competitive reasons
14% are dissatisfied with the product or service
68% quit because of an *attitude of indifference* toward the customer
    by the owner, manager or employee!

The consequences of poor customer service go well beyond having people leave your business. If one person is dissatisfied with your product or service, they will complain to approximately 10 people and the bad news about your business just keeps snowballing. Eventually, no matter how well you advertise your product or service, very few will do business with you.

To make sure you stay customer-oriented, focus on these definitions:

⇨ Treat people the way you want to be treated, but even more important, how *they* want to be treated.

⇨ Give customers what they want, when they want it and how they want it.

⇨ Good communication and human relations skills = Good customer service.

MARKETING BOOT CAMP

Success   #**74**   Strategy

5 Steps For Keeping Customers And Getting Referrals For Life

To get new customers, keep the ones you already have, and increase your referrals, here are five strategies to follow:

1. **Be Reliable.** First, you must determine what reliability means in your business. In other words, what is important in the eyes of your customers? For example, Federal Express is committed to the goal of "no service failures." This means that reliability is defined as delivering all priority packages by 10:30 a.m. the next day. Even though each business will have a different concept of reliability, there are basic rules that relate to every business.

    ⇨ *Do what you say you're going to do.*
    ⇨ *Do it when you say you're going to do it.*
    ⇨ *Do it right the first time.*
    ⇨ *Get it done on time.*

2. **Be Responsive.** Responsiveness means being accessible and willing to help customers whenever there is a problem. It also means keeping them informed and providing the services as soon as possible. For example, one cold evening Arnold's heating went out. He called a local heating company that promptly sent a repairman. Within one hour the unit was working. About an hour later he received a call asking if he was satisfied with the service. Several days later, Arnold received a thank you note and a decal displaying the company's name and telephone number. When he has a heating or cooling problem, guess which company he calls?

3. **Be Credible.** One area customers and potential customers look at when dealing with various companies is the trust, confidence and knowledge they demonstrate about their products or service. For instance, The United States Chamber of Commerce Department has instituted a hot-line phone number in which each person is trained to answer whatever questions are asked. And, as an example of both responsiveness and credibility, American Express has an 800 number reserved for customer complaints. If you call with a dispute about your bill, this number is answered by people with the authority to issue an immediate credit until the problem is resolved.

4. **Watch Your Appearance.** You've no doubt heard the saying, "Don't judge a book by its cover." Well, guess what? Everybody really does! Although appearances can be deceiving, customers quickly draw definitive conclusions about your quality of service based on what they see. If a bathroom is dirty in a restaurant, many people will wonder about the quality of the meals. Or, as one airline executive mentioned, "Coffee stains on the flip-down tray mean (to the customer) that maybe we do our engine maintenance wrong." Conversely, when the appearance is right, customers will (sometimes subconsciously) associate this with the quality of your product or service.

5. **Be Empathetic.** To the extent that you treat someone as special and solve his or her unique problems, he or she will continue to be your customer. Empathy means putting yourself in your customer's shoes—trying to grasp his or her point of view and feel what he or she does. For example, in the Nordstroms department stores, salespeople keep personal notebooks and make an extra effort to call you by name when you visit. Nordstroms knows the personal touch is the selling touch.

MARKETING BOOT CAMP

Success #**75** Strategy

Guidelines To Help You Stay Customer-Focused

To stay on the right track, ask yourself the following questions:

Is my service or product the best it can be?

Am I prepared to handle an increase in clients or customers smoothly and efficiently?

Is my pricing clear and fair so there are no misunderstandings?

Are my clients, suppliers and employees treated as honestly and fairly as possible?

If my clients, suppliers and employees do not agree with me or have questions, am I easily accessible? Do I take advantage of pagers, car phones and other time-saving devices?

Do I keep in contact with my clients on a regular basis?

Do my clients and prospective clients know as much as they want about my products, services and operations?

Can clients locate and reach my business with ease?

If clients have concerns about my services do they feel that I will listen to their problems and concerns?

Do I plan and carry out marketing activities on a regular basis? Too many business people are arbitrary in their marketing decisions and only market when business is slow. You need to always market your business to keep it on track.

MARKETING BOOT CAMP

Success   #**76**   Strategy

Perception Is Reality . . .
How Your Customers See You

During and after performing a service or providing a product, always follow up. By following up with our customers we can handle any possible problems and enhance the quality and frequency of future business. Ask yourself and your customers the following questions:

How well do we deliver what we promise?

How often do we do things right the first time?

How often do we do things right on time?

How quickly do we respond to your requests for service?

How accessible are we when you need to contact us?

How helpful and polite are we?

How well do we speak your language?

How hard do you think we work at keeping you a satisfied customer?

How much confidence do you have in our products or services?

How well do we understand and try to meet your special needs and requests?

Overall, how would you rate the appearance of our facilities, products and people?

Overall, how would you rate the quality of our service?

Overall, how would you rate the quality of our service compared to our competitors?

How willing would you be to recommend us?

How willing would you be to buy from us again?

MARKETING BOOT CAMP

Success   #**77**   Strategy

All Clients Are *Not* Created Equal

Our present and future success is directly related to the company we keep. Although it's tempting to take every client that walks through the door, it may not be in our best interest to do so. Choosing the right clients can enhance the speed and quality of our ultimate success. When looking at potential clients ask yourself these six questions:

1. **Do They Have Realistic Expectations?** One potential client of ours assumed that if he consulted with us for two hours he would go from a beginning non-paid speaker to one earning thousands of dollars a speech almost immediately. If his expectations were not met he would be very unhappy and surely let everyone know about it.

2. **Is There Good Chemistry?** In other words, how well do you get along with your client? Your work will be much more rewarding both personally and financially.

3. **Is the Work Challenging?** Remember the saying, "Do what you love and the money will follow"? It's true.

4. **Do They Pay on Time?** If clients start questioning your fees and making excuses . . . beware! Remember the #1 reason for business failure is poor cash flow.

5. **Do They Have Additional Needs?** It's six times more expensive to get new clients than to retain a current client.

6. **Do They Have Referrals for Future Work?** One client who hired us for presentation skills training continually refers us to others. Although he didn't have additional needs, his referrals have provided us with an income stream over 10 times the amount he paid us.

MARKETING BOOT CAMP

Success #**78** Strategy

How To Deal With Differing Communication Styles

To persuade and influence others to your way of thinking you need to adapt your communication methods (not your values) to the communication styles they feel are important. There are four prominent communication styles. To determine yours, take the following test.

1. Circle all the letters correlating to the adjectives that best describe you at work.
2. Add up all the A's P's T's and D's.
3. Look for areas where certain letters are more predominant than others.
4. Generally, if you have six or more in any area you have some of the characteristics of that area.
5. Remember, this is our predominant style and we are a little bit of each one.
6. To deal effectively with other people, review the following pages on divergent characteristics and how to deal with them.

P	Enthusiastic	A	Reserved
A	Warm	P	Sociable
T	Disciplined	P	Well liked
T	Precise	P	Excitable
D	Demeaning	D	Impatient
D	Aggressive	T	Analytic
D	Competitive	T	Questioning
T	Cautious	T	Critical
A	Calm	D	Controls conversation
A	Avoids conflict	D	Requires facts
P	Persuasive	D	Reaches quick decisions
T	Research oriented	P	Emotional
T	Serious	P	Playful
D	Decisive	A	Passive
P	Spontaneous	A	Shy
D	Risk-taker	T	Thorough
A	Loyal	T	Deliberate
P	Uninhibited	D	Firm
T	Detail oriented	D	Highly assertive
D	Stubborn	P	Political
D	Hard driving	P	Dynamic
T	Methodical	T	Careful
D	Bold	D	Controlling
D	Quick result getter	A	Tolerant
D	Direct	T	Well organized
A	Relaxed	P	Extroverted
T	Persistent	T	Worrier
A	Agreeable	A	Supportive
T	Unemotional	P	Impulsive
P	Exciting	A	Compliant
P	Convincing	D	Tough
D	Outspoken	P	Fun loving
A	Laid back	T	Prudent
T	Aloof	P	Energetic
T	Stuffy	D	Hard driving
P	High Energy	T	Reaches decisions slowly

Courtesy of Career Track Seminars.

How To Deal With Differing Communication Styles

Mirror and lead them! Mirror their behaviors and profiles, and display what they consider to be important communication ingredients and you will lead them to your way of thinking.

PROMOTERS	HOW TO DEAL WITH PROMOTERS
Verbal/vocal behaviors: They speak quickly and respond quickly, tend to be verbose and descriptive rather than economical in use of language. They use stories and anecdotes. They use vocal variety and their tone is generally optimistic.	Speak at their rate of speed. Use colorful language. Use stories and anecdotes. Use vocal inflection. Keep the vocabulary and tone optimistic.
Nonverbal behaviors: They are informal, friendly, stimulating and are political creatures. They deal well with people and thoroughly enjoy the contact. They throw themselves into it and are dynamic, energetic, enthusiastic, even charismatic. They lean forward when speaking, engage in direct eye contact, use facial expressions liberally, gesture to reinforce ideas and have relaxed posture.	Smile. Be enthusiastic and energetic. Use your body and face. Add movement to your presentation. Gesture animatedly.
Recognition profile: They are well liked, positive, think and present in "big picture" terms, like contact with people, feel bored and constrained by the routine, excited by the unstructured situation, do not enjoy working in isolation. They are impulsive and emotional. They are never bland and enjoy recognition and being noticed.	Downplay the routine. Play up the excitement of something new. Recognize them. Notice them.
Weaknesses: 1) While focusing on the "big picture," they tend to miss, even avoid, the details. They view deadlines and step-by-step, day-by-day instructions as boring and unchallenging. They see "visions." 2) They believe an important part of an encounter is "social lubrication"* and sometimes emphasize that to the point of annoyance for others. Not everyone believes in or needs social lubrication. *Social lubrication: How was your vacation? How is your family? Etc.*	Don't get bogged down in details. They'll be bored. Present "big pictures" and "visions." Be a motivating speaker. Social lubrication is especially important in smaller presentations and critical in 1-to-1. It builds the relationship, which is what promoters believe is the essential ingredient in business relationships.

DIRECTORS	HOW TO DEAL WITH DIRECTORS
Verbal/vocal behavior: They speak quickly and take direct action. They will take risks. They use forceful, direct language and specialize in facts, data, statistics. They are bottom line. Their voices are usually controlled, measured and more monotonous.	Speak at their rate of speed. Use direct language. Present facts, data, statistics. Present bottom line evidence. Control your voice, be louder, controlled, measured, more monotone. Avoid social lubrication.
Nonverbal behavior: They are more formal, competitive, businesslike and take charge. They like control. They deal civilly but directly with people. However, in crisis, they will act harshly, if need be, and let the chips fall where they may. They lean forward to make a point, engage in direct eye contact. Their body is rigid and formal. Their facial expression and body moves are controlled.	Control your facial expressions. Be more formal. Lean forward. Point. Gesture forcefully. Use direct eye contact.
Profile: They are feared by some and respected by others. They are recognized by an ability to get things done. They react swiftly, take direct action. "Let's get on with it" is their motto. They need control, action and insist upon results. They are risk-takers. If bureaucracies are in their way, they will find a way under, over, around or through and get results.	Show them a way to get it done. They are ultimate pragmatists and respect this.
Weaknesses: 1) If pushed, they will say the hard thing, even if feelings are hurt. 2) They are extremely competitive and can focus on immediate problem and lose sight of "big picture."	Keep in control if pressed by them, or you will be in a verbal death match and not persuade them. Focus on the common good, need for cooperation and defuse the negative competitive factor.
THINKERS	HOW TO DEAL WITH THINKERS
Verbal/vocal behaviors: They speak slowly and deliberately. Their language is careful, statements are fewer. They speak in a monotone and focus on data, facts and especially details.	Slow down your rate of speaking and match theirs carefully. Weigh your language so it is precise and coincides with the vocabulary of a Thinker. Limited vocal expression. Present data, facts. Be up to date, accurate and have the details right. Don't make a mistake or you lose credibility.
Nonverbal behaviors: They do not particularly enjoy dealing with people. Facts and data are certain. People are not, so posture is generally rigid. Eye contact is not direct. Their face shows little in the way of emotion. It is controlled. They don't point and present little in the way of gestures. "Life would be better if I didn't have to deal with people."	Rigid posture and controlled facial expression. Limit gestures and body moves. Use indirect eye contact.

Profile: They are sometimes perceived as negative people because they are always asking questions or setting up "hypothetical roadblocks." This is just their attempt to get all the facts and deal with all possible scenarios, so they can put together the best program. They are slow decision-makers, because they are cautious, organized, precise and detail-oriented.	Build your credibility and be prepared to answer all questions and provide facts, data and details, so they can make a decision.
Weaknesses: They are indecisive and sometimes suffer from "analysis paralysis."	
ACCOMMODATORS	HOW TO DEAL WITH ACCOMMODATORS
Verbal/vocal behavior: They speak slowly and are generally unhurried in their reactions. They are great listeners, and their language is supportive and non-controversial. They use vocal variety and present stories, examples and anecdotes.	Slow down your rate of speed. Use non-inflammatory, conciliatory language. Employ the full range of vocal variety. Present stories, examples and anecdotes.
Nonverbal behavior: They truly enjoy people, but they are shy. At meetings, they often don't speak out. They give indirect eye contact, lean back, do not gesture very much, but appear relaxed.	Smile. Lean back, don't be forceful. Relax. Use indirect eye contact.
Profile: They have a high need for a cooperative environment. They dislike conflict. They are the most loyal people in the organization and generally know the environment and like the parameters they have. They have a need for relationships and are strongly supportive team players.	
Weaknesses: They may not change, because change is too discomforting, the status quo is safe.	Show them the change is a functional imperative for survival. If this is not possible, show them how change will improve the organization and not jeopardize their position or status. In fact, it is even more persuasive to show them that their security in the organization will be enhanced by the change and then tell them how they can operate in the new situation.

Courtesy of Career Track Seminars.

MARKETING BOOT CAMP

Success #**79** Strategy

KWK . . . Kill Your Customers With Kindness

According to *U.S. News and World Report,* "Americans are ruder than ever." Simple kindness and good manners can greatly enhance your opportunity to win new customers and keep the customers you already have. Disneyland says it best in a statement they make to new employees. "We love to entertain Queens and Kings, but the vital thing to remember is this, *every* guest receives the VIP treatment. It's not just important to be friendly and courteous to the public . . . it's essential! At Disneyland we get tired, but never bored. And even if it's a rough day we appear happy. You've got to have an honest smile. It's got to come from within. To accomplish this, you've got to develop a sense of humor and a genuine interest in people. If nothing else helps, remember that you get paid for smiling."

No matter how busy you are, you must take time to make the other person feel important.

Mary Kay Ash, Founder, Mary Kay Cosmetics

You can foul up on almost anything and you'll get another chance. But if you screw up, even a little bit, on people management, you're gone. That's it, top performers or not.

IBM Executive

You can make more friends in two months by becoming interested in other people than you can in two years by trying to get people interested in you.

Dale Carnegie

MARKETING BOOT CAMP

Success #**80** Strategy

The 10 Commandments
Of Human Relations

1. SPEAK TO PEOPLE—THERE IS NOTHING SO NICE AS A CHEERFUL GREETING.

2. CALL PEOPLE BY NAME—THE SWEETEST MUSIC TO ANYONE'S EARS IS THE SOUND OF HIS OR HER NAME.

3. HAVE HUMILITY—THERE IS SOMETHING TO BE LEARNED FROM EVERY LIVING THING.

4. BE FRIENDLY—IF YOU WOULD HAVE A FRIEND, BE ONE.

5. BE CORDIAL—SPEAK AND ACT AS IF EVERYTHING YOU DO IS A PLEASURE.

6. BE SINCERELY INTERESTED IN OTHERS—YOU CAN LIKE ALMOST EVERYBODY IF YOU TRY.

7. BE GENEROUS WITH PRAISE AND CAUTIOUS WITH CRITICISM.

8. GIVE YOUR WORD—THEN KEEP IT.

9. BE CONSIDERATE OF THE FEELINGS OF OTHERS.

10. BE ALERT TO GIVE SERVICE—WHAT COUNTS MOST IN LIFE IS WHAT WE DO FOR OTHERS.

MARKETING BOOT CAMP

Success   #**81**   Strategy

It's Not That People Are *Difficult*, They're Just *Different*

By handling "difficult" people the right way, we will keep our "hard won" clients and the goodwill that goes with them. When dealing with "difficult people" follow these rules:

1. **Realize That People Who Are Angry Feel Justified in Their Anger**—Whether it's a perception or reality there is a "real" reason for their anger.
2. **Avoid Anger in Yourself**—Angry exchanges change few minds.
3. **Ask Questions**—Make sure you get to the real reason for the anger.
4. **Show Empathy**—Put yourself in the other person's shoes. Show empathy by saying such statements as "If I were in your shoes, I'd feel the same way" or "If I believed that, I'd probably feel the same way." Notice that neither of these statements says that you agree with the person. The only thing you're saying is that if you saw the situation the same way they did that's how you would feel.
5. **Listen**—Many times people just want to be listened to. When you listen they tend to calm down. Also by listening you find out what the real problems are.
6. **Take Responsibility for the Conflict**—Realize that something you did or didn't do caused the conflict to take place. If you are at fault, admit it.

7. **Summarize the Needs and Desires of Both Parties**—clarify the argument.

8. **Ask What You Can Do to Resolve the Disagreement**—By asking this you show that you want to be helpful and that you value the relationship. It's also surprising that when you seek a resolution, most people will just want to be treated fairly and won't "ask for the world."

9. **Choose Time and Place Carefully**—If you're going to get into a confrontation, make sure it's in private and pick a time when they will be most relaxed.

10. **Paraphrase What Has Been Said**—Repeat back what has been said to make sure you're both clear on what the real conflict is.

11. **Don't Interrupt**—Rapport, sensitivity, closeness and commitment are all killed.

12. **Mention Their Name**—If you're dealing with someone who is yelling at you, mention their name over and over again. This way you can add in what you want to say.

13. **Don't Accept It**—There are times when verbal abuse is uncalled for. It's at these times that it is apporpriate for you to tell them that their behavior is inappropriate and you won't accept it.

MARKETING BOOT CAMP

Success   #**82**   Strategy

Turn Complaints Into Opportunities

"I always view problems as opportunities in work clothes."
— HENRY J. KAISER

Unfortunately, many of us see customer complaints as problems or threats. Successful marketers view complaints as opportunities to improve their products or services and to keep customers coming back.

Look at your current system (you do have one don't you?) for handling complaints and answer the following questions?

What are the main reasons for complaints?

How are complaints handled?

Looking at the system from the *customer's point of view*, what should be changed?

What money and management resources are available to develop and/or maintain your customer complaint system?

Does your present service system deliver on its promise?

How does your present complaint system compare with those of your competitors?

To turn complaints into opportunities, do whatever it takes to satisfy the client. If one person is dissatisfied with your product/service, they then tell 10 others how bad you are. To make matters worse, these people tell even more. Also, only 2% of the people ever complain, the other 98% just tell everyone how bad you are.

When people complain, ask the question, "What can we do to satisfy you?" Follow through with their suggestion (immediately) and they'll not only not tell others how bad you are, but they'll tell everyone how good you are!

MARKETING BOOT CAMP

Success #**83** Strategy

Under Promise And Over Deliver . . . Exceeding Client Expectations

"There's no traffic jam on the extra mile." — ANONYMOUS

Too many individuals and companies pay lip service about providing exceptional service. In reality, most offer only the minimum service required.

If value equals benefits vs. cost, then value-added marketing means *exceeding* client expectations. Value is a personal perception. When people *perceive* they are getting more than they bargained for, they'll buy from you. Here are several examples to jump-start your thinking for adding *value* to whatever you're selling. These are subtle, yet powerful marketing strategies that motivate people to buy again and again:

1. A baby foods manufacturer provides a toll-free hotline where parents can ask questions about their baby's nutritional needs.
2. Companies are sponsoring our *Marketing Boot Camp Seminars* to provide their key customers and prime prospects with marketing information to help them prosper. Some will give attendees our book as a complimentary gift. Others will offer a free book to anyone opening a new account.
3. Several auto manufacturers now provide 24-hour roadside service 365 days a year to new vehicle owners.
4. A major food chain offers frequent shopper discounts and $25 to anyone who has to wait in line with more than three people in it.
5. Rental car companies now provide convenient automatic check-in and check-out. One company even picks up and drops off clients!
6. L. L. Bean's legendary "no questions asked" return policy.

A final point: People will not always understand or appreciate the extras you provide. So it's your job to tell them. What value-added promises can you offer your prospects and customers?

MARKETING BOOT CAMP

Success #**84** Strategy

18 *"Little Things"* You Can Do To Keep Customers Happy

It doesn't take much to separate you from your competition. The key to success lies in doing a lot of little things right. Below are 18 proven strategies to help you stand out in the crowded marketplace.

- ➭ Always call back when you say you will.
- ➭ Don't use call waiting. Give your full attention to each client.
- ➭ Give the customer something "extra." Go above and beyond what they expect.
- ➭ Send handwritten thank you cards to your clients and potential clients.
- ➭ Use your customers' products and services.
- ➭ Promote your customers' products and services to others.
- ➭ Kill them with Kindness (KWK).
- ➭ Follow up with clients by phone.
- ➭ Give guarantees.
- ➭ Do whatever you can to make your clients' lives easier.
- ➭ Remember names.
- ➭ Don't oversell your products and services. This is a sure way to generate negative talk.
- ➭ Keep in contact.
- ➭ Be enthusiastic—if *you* aren't no one else will be.
- ➭ Avoid arguments.
- ➭ Don't try to impress others. Let them impress you.
- ➭ Learn to like yourself. Others will respond to you the way you respond to yourself.
- ➭ Be positive. Positive people attract others; negative people repel others.

MARKETING BOOT CAMP

Success #**85** Strategy

The Secret Success Ingredient—YOU!

"It is our attitude at the beginning of a difficult undertaking which, more than anything else, will determine its successful outcome."— WILLIAM JAMES

Your attitude influences your internal communication which influences your external communication. How you see the world has a definite effect on how you come across to others. . . . And since you're really selling yourself, how others see you can make the difference between success and failure. To improve your attitude, there are three steps to follow:

1. Flipside Exercise—*No matter what happens, always look at the positive side of things. The following are some examples.*

I don't like my job	Flipside	*I at least have a job*
I put a dent in my new car	Flipside	*Now, I don't have to worry about it.*
My sales are off	Flipside	*At least I'm healthy enough to seek clients*

   Now list your "problems" and the flipside strategy you'll use:

   _____ Flipside _____
   _____ Flipside _____

2. Focus on what really counts—*Too many times we focus so much on our problems that we forget about all we have to be thankful about. List the five things in your life that really make it worthwhile.*

   _____
   _____
   _____
   _____
   _____

3. Simplify your life—*Look at all the areas where you can simplify your life. By doing this your outlook improves and you become more effective and efficient. For example, by cleaning off your desk, you don't seem as overwhelmed and you become calmer when dealing with clients. List five areas where you can simplify.*

_____

_____

_____

This final success strategy depends entirely on you and what you do with the insights and knowledge you've gleaned from this book and the lessons you've learned over a lifetime.

Many people talk about succeeding but few actually "do." Winners are the ones who "walk the talk" and do what others will not do. Perseverance pays. The most successful people are the ones who can suffer personal and professional setbacks, make a quick recovery and keep moving forward.

Some of the strategies in *Marketing Boot Camp* will prove more effective for you than others. Because 80% of your successes will come from 20% of your efforts, we urge you to invest the most "sweat equity" in the strategies that play to your personal strengths.

Act now! Many more business victories are won on attitude and action than on knowledge and talent. The essential ingredients to your marketing success are determination, commitment, enthusiasm, communication and disciplined *action*. Once you begin to implement and sustain the *The "9/18" Relationship Marketing System* and its accompanying arsenal of tools and techniques, you *will* reap the rewards.

Yet no one is immune to difficulties. Peaks and valleys are not optional experiences in marketing and sales. When you're feeling up, share it with others. When you're feeling low or unsure about any of the concepts in this book, dear reader, know that you have two friends who genuinely want to help you reach your goals and aspirations. Our phone numbers can be found on the following pages.

We wish you continued success in taking command of your business, your marketing and your financial future.

Arnold Sanow

Speaker • Trainer • Author • Consultant

Arnold Sanow, MBA, is one of America's leading authorities in the area of business development and personal effectiveness.

Whether you're looking for a powerful keynote, seminar or training program, Arnold is the right choice! His customized presentations are fast-paced, energetic, high-content and fun. But most of all, Arnold's sessions contain solid "how to" information that can be used immediately.

Arnold has given over **1,800 paid presentations and consults** with a variety of companies, associations and governmental organizations throughout the USA and overseas.

Arnold's speaking and training engagements have included such organizations as:

AT&T
C-SPAN
PBS
National Association of Credit
  Management
American Red Cross
American University
U.S. Navy
U.S. Department of Commerce
National Glass Association
American Association of Art
  Museum Directors
National Solid Waste Management
  Association
Meeting Planners International

American Indian Heritage
  Foundation
SkillPath Seminars
Boston Society of Architects
Harvard Club
Health Management Associates
National Institutes of Health
National Homebuilders Association
National Office Machine Dealers
  Association
Delphi International
Checkoslovakia (Government)
World Trade Center of Trinidad
  and Tabago
AND MORE!

Arnold's most requested topics include:

- *Communicate Like a Pro*
- *How to Make Powerful Presentations*
- *How to Provide Exceptional Customer Service*
- *Marketing Professional Services*
- *Marketing & Publicity on a Low Budget*
- *Skills for Success*
- *No Time to Kill . . . Managing Multiple Priorities*
- *Managing and Leading People*
- *Secrets of Successful Entrepreneurs*
- *How to Become a Successful Consultant and Speaker*

Arnold is a frequent guest on radio, television and in the print media. He is the author of the best-selling book, **"You Can Start Your Own Business"** and has been featured on such shows as the **CBS Evening News with Dan Rather,** *USA Today, Entrepreneur Magazine* and others. He is a regular columnist for the *Washington Business Advisor* and former talk show host of the radio show, "It's Your Business." Arnold is an adjunct professor at Georgetown University and President of The Business Source, Inc., a Business Development and Training Company.

Arnold lives in Vienna, Virginia with his wife Nancy and son, Stevie.

For more information on making your next event a memorable one, call Arnold today!

The Business Source, Inc.—703-255-3133

J. Daniel McComas

Speaker • Author • Copywriter • Consultant

*Here's How Dan Can Help You Attract More Customers And
Generate Higher Profits.*

Presentations and Training

When it comes to marketing and sales, speaking and training, Dan
McComas is widely sought for his relevant, high-content and dynamic
keynote and seminar programs. Dan's practical "how to" presentations
entertain, energize and empower his audiences to immediately implement
strategies necessary to profit in any economic environment. His "in the
trenches" insights and high-energy talks will make your meeting an event
to remember.

Dan's most requested programs include:

⇨ *Marketing Boot Camp*
⇨ *Network Your Way To Success*
⇨ *How To Unlock Your Creative Genius*
⇨ *Marketing And Publicity On A Shoestring*
⇨ *How To Write The Million Dollar Sales Letter*
⇨ *Supercharge Yourself! The Seven Secrets of Powerful
Self-Promotion*
⇨ *Speaking And Writing For Fame And Fortune*

Copywriting/Graphic Design Services

Dan and his associates have made millions of dollars for their clients by
writing benefit-rich, client-centered, results-driven copy that motivates
prospects to **buy now** and customers to **buy again fast**! His a la carte or
comprehensive campaign copywriting services include sales letters, ads
for broadcast and print media, brochures, flyers, postcards, news releases
and media kits. He can also create a cohesive visual identity for all of your
marketing communications through his Macintosh graphic design and
printing services. Additional services include: Media Planning and Buy-

ing, Public Relations, Photography, Trade Show Exhibits, Music, News-letters and "Second Opinion" copywriting evaluations.

Dan is president of **The International Marketing Institute,** a di-rect response marketing, training and consulting firm based in Silver Spring, Maryland. He consults with individuals, small businesses, profes-sional service firms, trade and professional associations and Fortune 500 companies. Additionally, he has taught marketing communications and advertising courses at The University of Maryland, The Montgomery College Small Business Development Center, and First Class, an adult education center.

Dan has a broad business and communications background as an advertising agency writer, trade association executive director, musician, and television news reporter and anchor for ABC and NBC affiliate sta-tions. He is a member of The National Speaker's Association, The Ameri-can Society For Training and Development, and is listed in "Who's Who In Advertising."

Dan lives in Kensington, Maryland with his wife, Erin and "my three sons," Matt, Alan and Jesse. For a free copy of his *Unfair Advantage Marketing Success Guide* packed with profitable recommendations for generating new and repeat business, or for information on Dan's speak-ing, writing and consulting services, call him today at **301-946-4284**!

You Can Become A Respected, Certified Marketing Consultant!

Earn $5,000–$30,000 Each Month In Your Own Seminar And Consulting Business!

Here's what you get to start making money immediately:

- License to present copyrighted *Marketing Boot Camp* workshops and speeches plus two other dynamic, in-depth seminars;
- Easy-to-follow turn-key operation—no prior experience is necessary;
- Fast, comprehensive training leading to the designation of Certified Marketing Consultant (CMC);
- Unlimited telephone support and consulting services;
- Ready-to-go proposals, sales letters, forms and contracts for your computer;
- Pre-written business "how to" articles you can publish under *your* by-line;
- Wholesale prices on student manuals, audio/video tapes and books for increased profits;
- Media contacts, clients;
- Work when you want to—full or part time;
- Low start-up investment of $10,997.

The income and prestige potential is limitless! To get your "unfair share" of the exploding multi-billion dollar training and consulting business, contact Dan McComas at (301) 946-4284 or Arnold Sanow, (703) 255-3133, at The International Marketing Institute for a free, no-obligation profit package.